Holly Jolly Christmas
In Plastic Canvas™

EDITED BY BOBBIE MATELA & LISA M. FOSNAUGH

Holly Jolly Christmas in Plastic Canvas

EDITOR	Bobbie Matela
ART DIRECTOR	Brad Snow
PUBLISHING SERVICES MANAGER	Brenda Gallmeyer
ASSOCIATE EDITOR	Lisa M. Fosnaugh
ASSISTANT ART DIRECTOR	Nick Pierce
COPY SUPERVISOR	Michelle Beck
COPY EDITOR	Judy Weatherford
TECHNICAL EDITOR	June Sprunger
GRAPHIC PRODUCTION SUPERVISOR	Ronda Bechinski
GRAPHIC ARTISTS	Debby Keel
	Edith Teegarden
PRODUCTION ASSISTANTS	Marj Morgan
	Judy Neuenschwander
PHOTOGRAPHY	Tammy Christian
	Don Clark
	Matthew Owen
	Jackie Schaffel
PHOTO STYLISTS	Tammy Nussbaum
	Tammy M. Smith
CHIEF EXECUTIVE OFFICER	David McKee
MARKETING DIRECTOR	Dwight Seward

Printed in China
First Printing: 2007
Library of Congress Control Number: 2006934884
Hardcover ISBN: 978-1-57367-260-3
Softcover ISBN: 978-1-57367-275-7

1 2 3 4 5 6 7 8 9

Celebrate!

Prepare for the jolliest time of the year with merry plastic canvas ideas by our favorite designers.

Create Joyful Tissue Toppers for every room of the house or to give as the perfect hostess gift.

Present Merry Gift Givers for a colorful and clever alternative to the usual gift wrappings.

Trim the tree with Festive Ornaments that will bring smiles to the faces of family and friends.

Have fun stitching our Ho, Ho, Ho designs, chosen for their jolly outook and the happiness they will bring to the festivities.

Warm up your home's surroundings with inspired designs to Deck the Halls and set the stage for a memorable Christmas.

Since plastic canvas projects can be stitched quickly, there's plenty of time to add cheer to your holiday celebrations with charming plastic canvas style.

Jolly Stitching!

Bobbie Matela

Lisa M Fosnaugh

Joyful Tissue Toppers

Merry Gift Givers

Festive Ornaments

Ho, Ho, Ho

Deck the Halls

Joyful Tissue Toppers

Whatever your holiday decorating style, tissue toppers are a quick and easy way to add a little Christmas cheer. From cute and whimsical to elegant and sophisticated, you'll feel joyful as you stitch each design in this chapter.

Wee Country Angels Ornaments & Topper

These sweet little angels are embellished with twine for a topper and ornament duo that will add country charm to your home.

DESIGNS BY JANELLE GIESE

Skill Level
Intermediate

Size
Topper: Fits boutique-style tissue box

Angels: 2⅜ inches W x 2¾ inches H (6cm x 7cm), including halo

Materials
- 2 sheets 7-count plastic canvas
- Coats & Clark Red Heart Classic worsted weight yarn Art. E267 as listed in color key
- Coats & Clark Red Heart Super Saver worsted weight yarn Art. E300 as listed in color key
- 2-ply jute twine as listed in color key
- DMC #3 pearl cotton as listed in color key
- DMC #5 pearl cotton as listed in color key
- DMC 6-strand embroidery floss as listed in color key
- #16 tapestry needle
- #20 tapestry needle
- ½ sheet antique white felt
- Invisible sewing thread
- Powder cosmetic blush
- Cotton swab
- Thick white glue

Tissue Topper
1. Cut one top and four sides from plastic canvas according to graphs (pages 9 and 10).
2. Stitch pieces following graphs, working uncoded areas with Aran fleck Continental Stitches.
3. When background stitching is completed, work very dark garnet and very dark gray green Backstitches.

4. Overcast inside edges of top with ranch red. Using linen, Whipstitch sides together, then Whipstitch sides to top; Overcast bottom edges.

Angels
1. Cut eight angels (four for each set) from plastic canvas according to graph (page 10). For angel ornaments, cut four pieces antique white felt slightly smaller than angels.

2. Stitch and Overcast one set of angels for tissue topper, working uncoded area on each face with tan Continental Stitches. Work wings with natural jute twine.
3. Stitch robes on angels as follows: gold angel with cornmeal and honey gold, green angel with teal and seafoam, ivory angel with off white and eggshell, red angel with ranch red and cardinal, Overcasting each robe with the darker color.
4. When background stitching is completed, work pearl cotton embroidery where indicated. For eye highlights, using #20 tapestry needle and ecru pearl cotton, bring needle up through center of French Knot, over edge and back down through same hole.
5. Using natural jute twine, work Laid Stitch portion of Couching Stitches on robes and heads; couch Laid Stitches with 2 plies medium mocha brown floss where indicated.
6. For each halo, knot ends of a 5-inch (12.7cm) length of jute twine together, forming a circle. Trim tails as needed. With knot behind head, glue halo in place (see photo).

7. Apply powdered blush to cheek areas with cotton swab.

8. Center and glue one angel to each side of tissue topper.

9. Repeat steps 2–7 for angel ornaments. Attach hangers to top back sides of angels, using desired length of invisible thread. Glue felt to back sides of angels over bottoms of halos and hangers. 🌿

COLOR KEY
TISSUE TOPPER

Yards	Worsted Weight Yarn
15 (13.8m)	■ Ranch red #332
61 (55.8m)	Uncoded areas are Aran fleck #4313 Continental Stitches
7 (6.5m)	⁄ Linen #330 Overcast and Whipstitch
	#3 Pearl Cotton
6 (5.5m)	✦ Very dark garnet #902 Backstitch
14 (12.9m)	✦ Very dark gray green #924 Backstitch

Color numbers given are for Coats & Clark Red Heart Super Saver worsted weight yarn Art. E300 and DMC #3 pearl cotton.

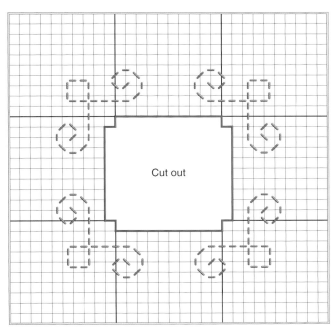

Wee Country Angels Topper Top
30 holes x 30 holes
Cut 1

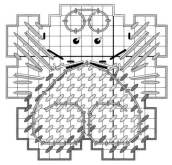

Wee Country Angel
15 holes x 15 holes
Cut 4 for each set,
Stitch 1 robe in each set for
gold, green, ivory and red angels

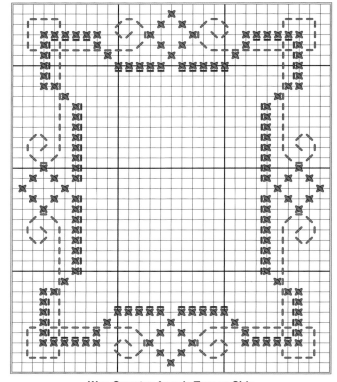

Wee Country Angels Topper Side
30 holes x 36 holes
Cut 4

COLOR KEY
ANGELS

Yards	Worsted Weight Yarn
6 (5.5m)	Uncoded areas are tan #334 Continental Stitches
	⁄ Tan #334 Overcast
	2-Ply Jute Twine
14 (12.9m)	☐ Natural
	⁄ Natural Laid Stitch of Couching Stitch
	#3 Pearl Cotton
2 (1.9m)	⁄ Ecru Backstitch and Straight Stitch
	#5 Pearl Cotton
2 (1.9m)	✏ Black brown #3371 Backstitch and Straight Stitch
	● Black brown #3371 French Knot
	6-Strand Embroidery Floss
1 (1m)	⁄ Medium mocha brown #3032 (2-ply) Couching Stitch
	Worsted Weight Yarn
Gold Angel	
2 (1.9m)	☐ Cornmeal #320
2 (1.9m)	■ Honey gold #645
Green Angel	
2 (1.9m)	■ Teal #48
2 (1.9m)	☐ Seafoam #684
Ivory Angel	
2 (1.9m)	☐ Off white #3
2 (1.9m)	■ Eggshell #111
Red Angel	
2 (1.9m)	☐ Ranch red 332
2 (1.9m)	■ Cardinal #917

Color numbers given are for Coats & Clark Red Heart Classic worsted weight yarn Art. E267 and Super Saver worsted weight yarn Art. E300, and DMC #5 pearl cotton and 6-strand embroidery floss.

COLOR KEY
TISSUE TOPPER

Yards	Worsted Weight Yarn
15 (13.8m)	■ Ranch red #332
61 (55.8m)	Uncoded areas are Aran fleck #4313 Continental Stitches
7 (6.5m)	⁄ Linen #330 Overcast and Whipstitch
	#3 Pearl Cotton
6 (5.5m)	✏ Very dark garnet #902 Backstitch
14 (12.9m)	⁄ Very dark gray green #924 Backstitch

Color numbers given are for Coats & Clark Red Heart Super Saver worsted weight yarn Art. E300 and DMC #3 pearl cotton.

Pocket Packs

Keep tissues handy in your purse or car by stowing travel-size packs in these miniature holders.

DESIGN BY MARY T. COSGROVE

Skill Level
Beginner

Size
Fits pocket-size tissues

Materials
- ¼ sheet white 7-count plastic canvas
- ½ sheet red 7-count plastic canvas
- ½ sheet green 7-count plastic canvas
- Uniek Needloft plastic canvas yarn as listed in color key
- #16 tapestry needle

Instructions

1. Cut one pocket front and back from red plastic canvas and one pocket front and back from green plastic canvas according to graphs (page 31), cutting out opening on front pieces only.

2. Cut four trim pieces from white plastic canvas according to graph (page 31).

3. Place white trim on fronts where indicated with blue lines. Using red yarn with green front and holly yarn with red front, work Cross Stitches through both layers of plastic canvas and French Knots in cut-out areas of trim pieces.

4. Using white throughout, Overcast inside edges on front pieces, then Whipstitch corresponding fronts and backs together around outside edges, catching ends of trim while Whipstitching.

5. Add tissues through opening in front.

GRAPHS ON PAGE 31

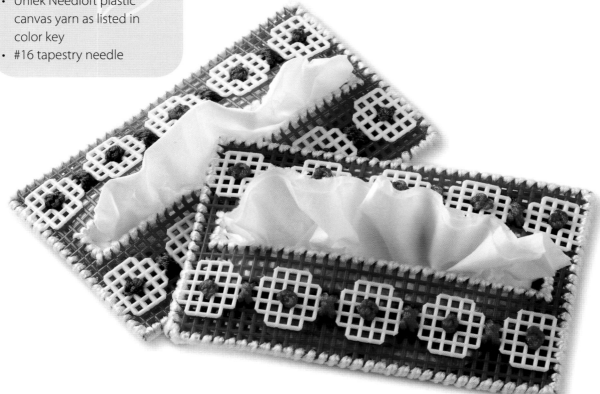

O Tannenbaum

Add a festive touch to your holiday decor with this topper that features a brightly trimmed tree, complete with garland and bows!

DESIGN BY NANCY DORMAN

Skill Level
Beginner

Size
Fits boutique-style tissue box

Materials
- 1½ sheets 7-count plastic canvas
- Worsted weight yarn as listed in color key
- 2.5mm Rainbow Gallery Plastic Canvas 10 Metallic Needlepoint Yarn as listed in color key
- #16 tapestry needle
- 4 yards (3.7m) red 6-strand embroidery floss
- 40 (3mm) gold beads
- Hand-sewing needle
- Dark green sewing thread
- Wax paper
- Craft glue

Project Note
Depending on size of boutique-style tissue box, this topper may be a very tight fit.

Instructions
1. Cut plastic canvas according to graphs (page 14).
2. Stitch pieces following graphs, working Smyrna Cross Stitch border first, then trees. Work uncoded backgrounds with ivory Continental Stitches.
3. When background stitching is completed, using gold metallic yarn throughout, work Backstitches just inside Smyrna Cross Stitch border. Work Laid Stitch portion of Couching Stitch for garland then secure with small Couching Stitches.
4. Attach gold beads to trees where indicated, using hand-sewing needle and green sewing thread.
5. Using red yarn throughout, Overcast inside edges of top and bottom edges of sides. Using regular Whipstitch (page 175) or Binding Stitch (page 14), stitch sides together, then stitch sides to top.
6. For red bows, cut floss in nine (15-inch/38.1cm) lengths and one 5-inch (12.7cm) length.
7. To stiffen floss, place glue between thumb and forefinger and slide down each length floss. Allow to dry on wax paper. Floss does not need to be completely stiff. Cut each 15-inch (38.1cm) length into three 5-inch (27.1cm) pieces, then tie all 28 lengths in very tiny bows; trim ends. Glue to sides where indicated. 🍂

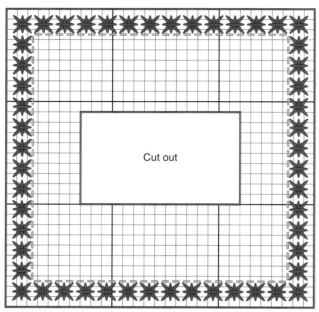

O Tannenbaum Top
29 holes x 29 holes
Cut 1

O Tannenbaum Side
29 holes x 37 holes
Cut 4

COLOR KEY		
Yards		**Worsted Weight Yarn**
50 (45.7m)	■	Red
35 (32m)	■	Dark green
1 (1m)	■	Light brown
50 (45.7m)		Uncoded areas are ivory Continental Stitches
		2.5mm Metallic Needlepoint Yarn
25 (22.9m)	⁄	Gold #PM51 Backstitch and Couching Stitch
	○	Attach gold bead
	●	Attach red bow

Color number given is for Rainbow Gallery Plastic Canvas 10 Metallic Needlepoint Yarn.

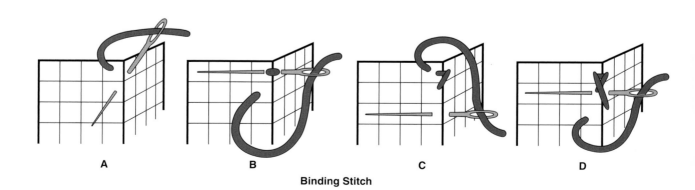

A   B   C   D

Binding Stitch

O Snowy Night

Snowflakes dance across the rich shades of blue on this icy set to create the look of a beautiful winter evening.

DESIGN BY ANGIE ARICKX

Skill Level
Beginner

Size
Fits family size tissue box

Materials
- 1½ sheets 7-count plastic canvas
- Coats & Clark Red Heart Super Saver weight yarn Art. E300 as listed in color key
- Uniek Needloft metallic craft cord as listed in color key
- #16 tapestry needle

Instructions
1. Cut plastic canvas according to graphs (pages 16 and 17).
2. Stitch pieces following graphs. Overcast inside edges on top with blue, and bottom edges of sides and ends with white.
3. Using soft navy, Whipstitch sides to ends, then Whipstitch sides and ends to top. 🦌

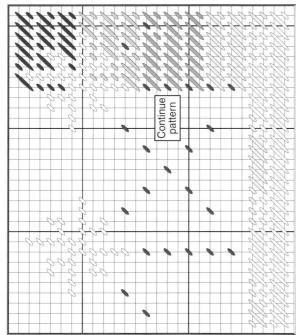

O Snowy Night End
32 holes x 27 holes
Cut 2

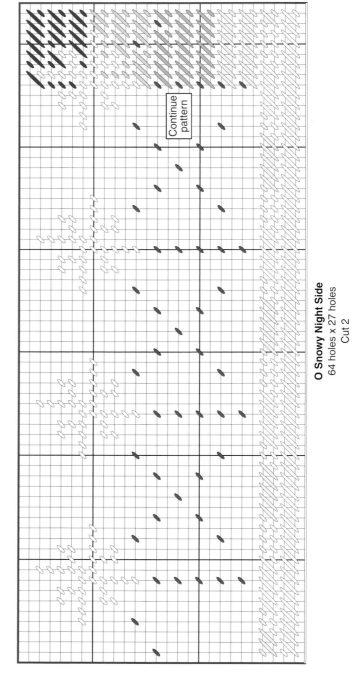

O Snowy Night Side
64 holes x 27 holes
Cut 2

COLOR KEY

Yards	Worsted Weight Yarn
15 (13.8m)	☐ White #311
19 (17.4m)	▨ Royal #385
21 (19.3m)	■ Soft navy #387
12 (11m)	☐ Delft blue #885
20 (18.3m)	▨ Blue #886
	Metallic Craft Cord
7 (6.5m)	■ White/silver #55008

Color numbers given are for Coats &
Clark Red Heart Super Saver worsted
weight yarn Art. E300 and Uniek
Needloft metallic craft cord.

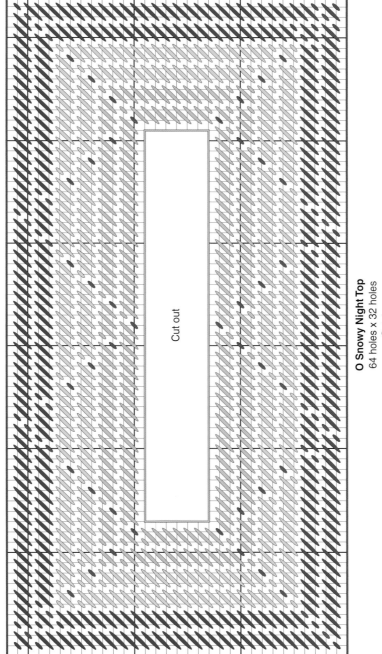

O Snowy Night Top
64 holes x 32 holes
Cut 1

Cut out

Frosty's Winter

Right at home in the cold, this darling snowman keeps warm with a fabric scarf.

DESIGN BY MICHELE WILCOX

Skill Level
Beginner

Size
Fits boutique-size tissue box

Materials
- 1½ sheets 7-count plastic canvas
- Uniek Needloft plastic canvas yarn as listed in color key
- #3 pearl cotton as listed in color key
- #5 pearl cotton as listed in color key
- #16 tapestry needle
- 4 (13 x 1½-inch/33cm x 3.8cm) strips calico fabric
- Hot-glue gun

Instructions
1. Cut plastic canvas according to graphs, cutting out holes on each side for scarf.

2. Stitch topper pieces following graphs, working uncoded areas with sail blue Continental Stitches.

3. When background stitching is completed, work pearl cotton embroidery where indicated.

4. Overcast inside edges on top and sides; Overcast bottom edges of sides.

5. For each side, thread ends of one fabric strip from back to front through holes at neck of snowman. Tie loosely in a knot on front; glue to secure.

6. Whipstitch sides together, then Whipstitch sides to top. ❦

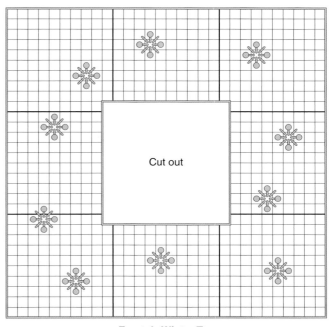

Frosty's Winter Top
30 holes x 30 holes
Cut 1

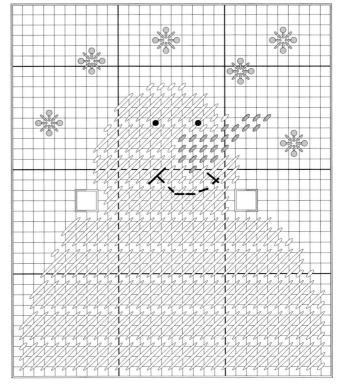

Frosty's Winter Side
30 holes x 36 holes
Cut 4

Deck the Halls Snowman

Christmas cheer abounds with a cheery snowman decorating the tree just in time for the holiday season.

DESIGN BY NANCY DORMAN

Skill Level
Beginner

Size
Fits boutique-style tissue box

Materials
- 2½ sheets 7-count plastic canvas
- Worsted weight yarn as listed in color key
- 2.5mm Rainbow Gallery Plastic Canvas 10 Metallic Needlepoint Yarn as listed in color key
- 6-strand embroidery floss as listed in color key
- #16 tapestry needle
- 9 inches (22.9cm) ⅛-inch/3mm-wide green satin ribbon
- 15 (5-inch/12.7cm) lengths ¹⁄₁₆-inch/1.5mm-wide maroon satin ribbon
- 15 (4mm) white pearl beads
- 12 gold confetti stars
- Orange hor d'oeuvre toothpick
- Hand-sewing needle
- Dark green sewing thread
- Hot-glue gun

Project Note
Depending on size of boutique-style tissue box, this topper may be a very tight fit.

Instructions
1. Cut plastic canvas according to graphs (pages 22 and 23).

2. Stitch sides and top following graphs. Overcast inside edges on top and bottom edges of sides. Using regular Whipstitch (page 175) or Binding Stitch (page 23), stitch sides together, then stitch sides to top.

3. Stitch and Overcast motif following graph, working uncoded areas on white background with white Continental Stitches and uncoded area on green background with green Continental Stitches.

4. When background stitching is completed, work black and maroon yarn embroidery following graph. Work leaves on hat with green floss Straight Stitches.

5. Using gold metallic yarn throughout, work French Knots on vest and hat. Work Straight Stitch for garland tail, then work Couching Stitches for garland.

6. Using hand-sewing needle and green sewing thread, attach white pearl beads to trees where indicated.

7. Tie green ribbon in a bow and glue to snowman where indicated. Tie maroon ribbon lengths in tiny bows, trimming ends. Glue bows and gold stars to tree where indicated.

8. For carrot nose, cut orange toothpick to desired length. Glue and insert toothpick in hole indicated.

9. Center snowman on one side of topper. Making sure bottom edges are even, secure in place with matching color of yarn used on snowman. 🍂

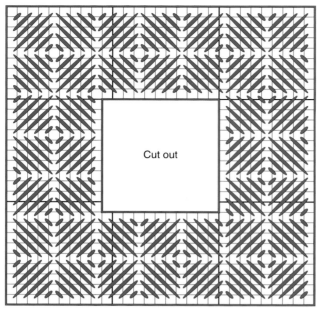

Deck the Halls Snowman Top
29 holes x 29 holes
Cut 1

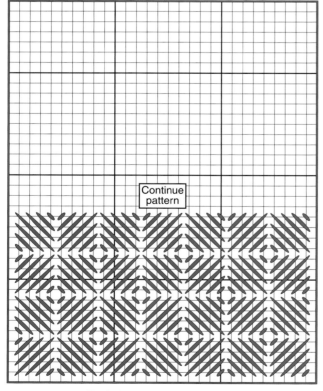

Continue
pattern

Deck the Halls Snowman Side
29 holes x 37 holes
Cut 4

COLOR KEY		
Yards		**Worsted Weight Yarn**
120 (110m)	■	Green
12 (11m)	■	Maroon
6 (5.5m)	■	Black
1 (1m)	☐	Light gray
		Uncoded areas on green background are green Continental Stitches
20 (18.3m)		Uncoded areas on white background are white Continental Stitches
	⁄	White Overcast
	／	Black Backstitch
	●	Maroon French Knot
	●	Black French Knot
5 (4.6m)		**2.5mm Metallic Needlepoint Yarn**
	☐	Gold #PM51
	⁄	Gold #PM51 Backstitch and Couching Stitch
1 (1m)	◐	Gold #PM51 French Knot
		6-Strand Embroidery Floss
	⁄	Green Straight Stitch
	○	Attach white pearl bead
	♥	Attach green ribbon bow
	▲	Attach maroon ribbon bow
	☆	Attach gold star
	◐	Attach nose

Color number given is for Rainbow Gallery Plastic Canvas 10 Metallic Needlepoint yarn

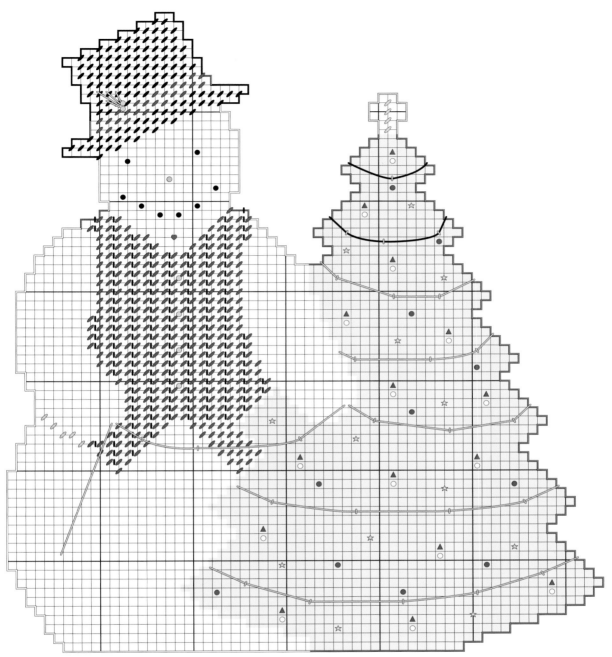

Deck the Halls Snowman Motif
64 holes x 71 holes
Cut 1

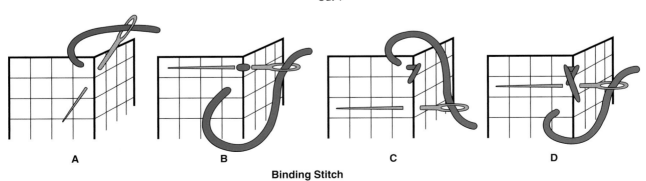

A   B   C   D

Binding Stitch

Victorian Poinsettia

Soft chenille yarn and metallic thread accents add to the elegant beauty of this festive topper.

DESIGN BY JANELLE GIESE

Skill Level
Advanced

Size
Fits boutique-style tissue box

Materials
- 1½ sheets Uniek Quick-Count black 7-count plastic canvas
- ¾ sheet Uniek Quick-Count burgundy 7-count plastic canvas
- Elmore-Pisgah Inc. Honeysuckle rayon chenille yarn as listed in color key
- Kreinik Heavy (#32) Braid as listed in color key
- Kreinik ⅛-inch Ribbon as listed in color key
- #16 tapestry needle
- 36 (5.5mm) Mill Hill old gold #05557 pebble beads from Wichelt Imports Inc.
- Thick white glue

Project Note
Use double strands of yarn (not graphed) when stitching with rayon chenille yarn.

Cutting & Stitching
1. Cut two sides, one back, one front, one top and one center base from black plastic canvas according to graphs (pages 26 and 27).

2. Following graphs (pages 26 and 27) and cutting away blue lines on center base rings, cut the following from burgundy plastic canvas:
8 large petals
8 medium petals
3 small petals
3 tiny petals
4 center base outer rings A
4 center base outer rings B
2 center base inner rings C
2 center base inner rings D
4 center base core rings E

3. Stitch front, back, sides and top following graphs, leaving center area indicated on front unworked, and filling in bottom portion of front around leaves with black Continental Stitches. Center base will remain unstitched.

4. When background stitching on topper pieces is completed, work gold braid Backstitches. Overcast inside edges on top with gold and bottom edges of sides with black.

5. Stitch and Overcast poinsettia petals with ruby and red Continental Stitches following graphs, closing darts (indicated with brackets) while stitching. Leave bottom edges of each petal unstitched.

6. Work red ribbon Straight Stitches over background stitching on large, medium and small petals.

Poinsettia Assembly

1. Using ruby, Whipstitch bottom edges of petals to unstitched center area of front where indicated, matching green, blue and orange lines and bright pink dots.

2. Using black, Whipstitch topper front and back to sides, then Whipstitch front to top. Using black and ruby, Whipstitch back and sides to top.

3. Using hunter green through step 8, Whipstitch bottom edges of center base outer rings A and B to edges on unstitched center base following Fig. 1.

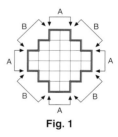

Fig. 1

4. Whipstitch side edges of supports on A and B pieces together, then Overcast top edges of supports. Do not Overcast bars extending above supports.

5. Following Fig. 2 (page 26), Whipstitch bottom edges of inner rings C and D to center base. Inner rings C and D are not Whipstitched together, and top of supports and bars extending above supports are

not Overcast. **Note:** *Rings A, B, C and D will lean outward from center.*

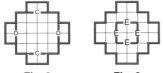

Fig. 2   Fig. 3

6. Work center stitch on core ring D supports, then Whipstitch side edges together, forming a square. Following Fig. 3, Whipstitch bottom edges to center base; Overcast top edges of supports. Bars extending above supports are not Overcast.

7. When all rings are attached to base, glue one pebble bead to each bar extending above supports. Allow to dry.

8. Place completed center base on front piece where indicated on graph and attach with a Cross Stitch at center of base. 🌿

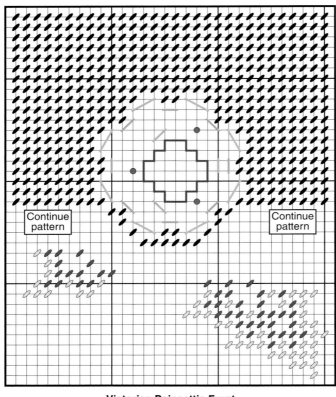

Continue pattern

Continue pattern

Victorian Poinsettia Front
31 holes x 37 holes
Cut 1

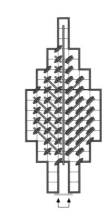

Victorian Poinsettia Large Petal
7 holes x 17 holes
Cut 8 from burgundy

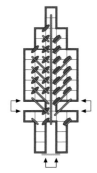

Victorian Poinsettia Medium Petal
5 holes x 14 holes
Cut 8 from burgundy

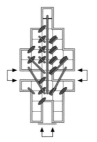

Victorian Poinsettia Small Petal
5 holes x 11 holes
Cut 3 from burgundy

Victorian Poinsettia Tiny Petal
3 holes x 8 holes
Cut 3 from burgundy

**Victorian Poinsettia
Center Base**
6 holes x 6 holes
Cut 1 from black

←— Support

**Center Base
Outer Ring A**
2 holes x 3 holes
Cut 4 from burgundy,
cutting away blue lines

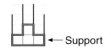
←— Support

**Center Base
Outer Ring B**
3 holes x 4 holes
Cut 4 from burgundy,
cutting away blue lines

←— Support

**Center Base
Inner Ring C**
2 holes x 3 holes
Cut 2 from burgundy,
cutting away blue lines

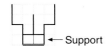
←— Support

**Center Base
Inner Ring D**
4 holes x 4 holes
Cut 2 from burgundy,
cutting away blue lines

←— Support

**Center Base
Core Ring E**
2 holes x 4 holes
Cut 4 from burgundy,
cutting away blue lines

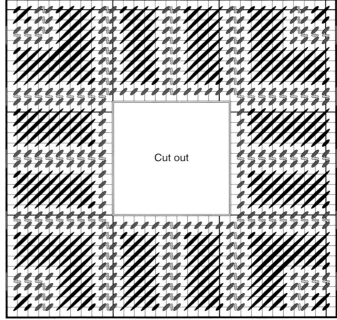

Cut out

Front Edge

Victorian Poinsettia Top
31 holes x 31 holes
Cut 1 from black

COLOR KEY

Yards	Rayon Chenille Yarn
8 (7.4m)	■ Hunter #19
6 (5.5m)	▨ Red #22
102 (93.3m)	■ Ruby #23
116 (106.1m)	■ Black #30
2 (1.9m)	□ Christmas green #37
	Heavy (#32) Braid
15 (13.8m)	⁄ Gold #002 Backstitch and Overcast
	¹/₈-Inch Ribbon
14 (12.9m)	⁄ Red #003 Straight Stitch
	⁄ Attach center base
	⁄ Attach large petal
	⁄ Attach medium petal
	⁄ Attach small petal
	● Attach tiny petal

Color numbers given are for Elmore-Pisgah
Honeysuckle rayon chenille yarn and Kreinik Heavy (#32)
Braid and ¹/₈-Inch Ribbon.

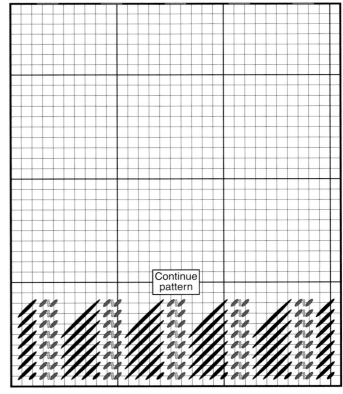

Continue
pattern

Victorian Poinsettia Side & Back
31 holes x 37 holes
Cut 3 from black

Peppermint & Ribbons

Yummy candy cane stripes are cleverly wrapped up with pretty green bows on this sweet tissue topper.

DESIGN BY JANELLE GIESE

Skill Level
Beginner

Size
Fits boutique-style tissue box

Materials
- 1½ sheets 7-count plastic canvas
- Coats & Clark Red Heart Classic worsted weight yarn Art. E267 as listed in color key
- Coats & Clark Red Heart Kids worsted weight yarn Art. E711 as listed in color key
- Kreinik Heavy (#32) Braid as listed in color key
- #16 tapestry needle
- 3 yards (2.8m) ⅛-inch/3mm-wide emerald green satin ribbon
- Thick white glue

Instructions

1. Cut plastic canvas according to graphs (page 30).

2. Stitch pieces following graphs, working uncoded areas with black Continental Stitches.

3. When background stitching is completed, work ruby braid Straight Stitches. At this time, do not work the ruby Straight Stitches that go over edges.

4. Using 2 plies lime, work Backstitches on top.

5. Using paddy green throughout, Overcast inside edges on top and bottom edges of sides. Whipstitch sides together. Using full strand lime, work Backstitches along Whipstitched edges.

6. Whipstitch sides to top following graphs, then complete ruby Straight Stitches on top, working over Whipstitched edges.

7. Cut ribbon in 12 (9-inch/23.3cm) lengths. Using photo as a guide, tie three lengths together in a bow and glue to one corner on top at green intersection. Repeat for remaining corners. ❧

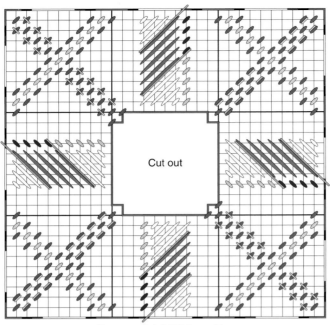

Peppermint & Ribbons Top
30 holes x 30 holes
Cut 1

COLOR KEY	
Yards	**Worsted Weight Yarn**
15 (13.8m)	☐ White #1
6 (5.5m)	☐ Silver #412
23 (21.2m)	■ Paddy green #686
6 (5.5m)	■ Cardinal #917
13 (11.9m)	■ Red #2390
10 (9.2m)	☐ Lime #2652
21 (19.3m)	Uncoded areas are black #12 Continental Stitches
	╱ Black #12 Whipstitch
	╱ Lime #2652 (4-ply) Backstitch
	╱ Lime #2652 (2-ply) Backstitch
7 (6.5m)	**Heavy (#32) Braid**
	╱ Ruby #061 Straight Stitch

Color numbers given are for Coats & Clark Red Heart Classic worsted weight yarn Art. E267 and Kids worsted weight yarn Art. E711, and Kreinik Heavy (#32) Braid.

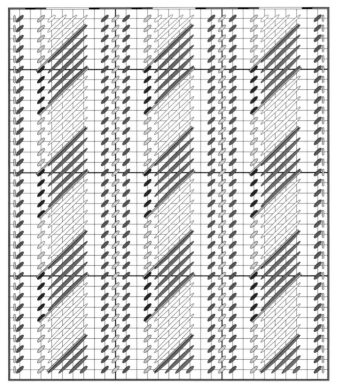

Peppermint & Ribbons Side
30 holes x 36 holes
Cut 4

Pocket Packs

CONTINUED FROM PAGE 11

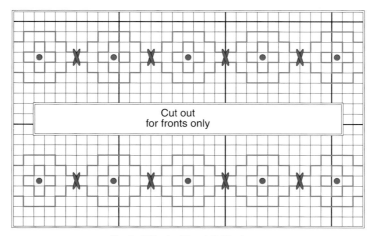

Pocket Packs Front & Back
33 holes x 21 holes
Cut 2 from green
Cut 2 from red
Stitch green front as graphed
Stitch red front with holly

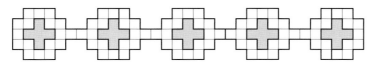

Pocket Packs Trim
33 holes x 5 holes
Cut 4 from white,
cutting away gray areas

COLOR KEY	
Yards	**Plastic Canvas Yarn**
3 (2.8m)	■ Red #01
3 (2.8m)	Holly #27
5 (4.6m)	⁄ White #41 Overcasting and Whipstitching
	⁄ Attach trim
Color numbers given are for Uniek Needloft plastic canvas yarn.	

Merry Gift Givers

Warm someone's heart when you present a thoughtful gift nestled inside a plastic canvas package made with love. You'll find the perfect design for gifts of all sizes!

Reindeer Stocking

Santa's favorite friend is ready to celebrate this holiday season with a festive garland decorated with sparkling beads.

DESIGN BY DEBRA ARCH

Skill Level
Beginner

Size
10½ inches W x 18½ inches H (26.7cm x 47cm)

Materials
- 2½ sheets 7-count plastic canvas
- 8 Uniek QuickShape plastic canvas hexagons
- Uniek Needloft plastic canvas yarn as listed in color key
- #16 tapestry needle
- 2 (¾-inch/1.9cm) round black shank buttons
- 1-inch (25mm) gold jingle bell
- 2 yards (1.9m) ½-inch/ 1.3cm-wide green garland
- 2 yards (1.9m) 10mm red bead garland
- 2 yards (1.9m) 4mm gold bead garland
- ½-inch bone ring
- Powder cosmetic blush
- Cotton swab
- Shank cutter
- Hot-glue gun

Cutting & Stitching
1. Cut front, back and antlers from plastic canvas according to graphs (pages 36 and 37), cutting away gray areas on hexagons for antlers.
2. Stitch pieces following graphs, using two stitches per hole for reindeer's hooves.
3. When background stitching is completed, work Straight Stitch on front between legs as graphed. On back, work Straight Stitch, 16 holes longer than front Straight Stitch, up to tail attachment.
4. Using sandstone throughout, Overcast top edge of back and around side and bottom edges of head from dot to dot, attaching jingle bell to tip of nose while Whipstitching.

Antler Assembly
1. Following assembly diagram (page 36), with right sides facing up, place one bottom antler over one top antler, keeping points ⅝ inch (1.6cm) apart; tack together with black yarn.
2. Repeat to make three more antler units.
3. Whipstitch wrong sides of two units together along all edges. Repeat for second antler.
4. Tack to top right side of body front where indicated with blue shading. Overcast body edges behind antlers.

Finishing
1. Wrap sandstone yarn five times around three fingers. Remove from fingers and tie in center with a 6-inch (15.2cm) length of sandstone yarn; cut loops to form hair tuft. Glue to top center front of head where indicated.
2. Repeat for tail, tacking to body back where indicated on graph.
3. Whipstitch wrong sides of front and back together around side and bottom edges following graph.
4. With right sides facing front, Whipstitch top edge of head to top edge of body front, Overcasting edges in front of antlers while Whipstitching.
5. Cut shanks from button and glue to head for eyes where indicated on graph.
6. Apply blush to cheeks with cotton swab where indicated with pink shading.
7. Fold green garland in half and twist together. Wrap red and gold bead garlands around green garland. Wrap around head and antlers as desired. 🦌

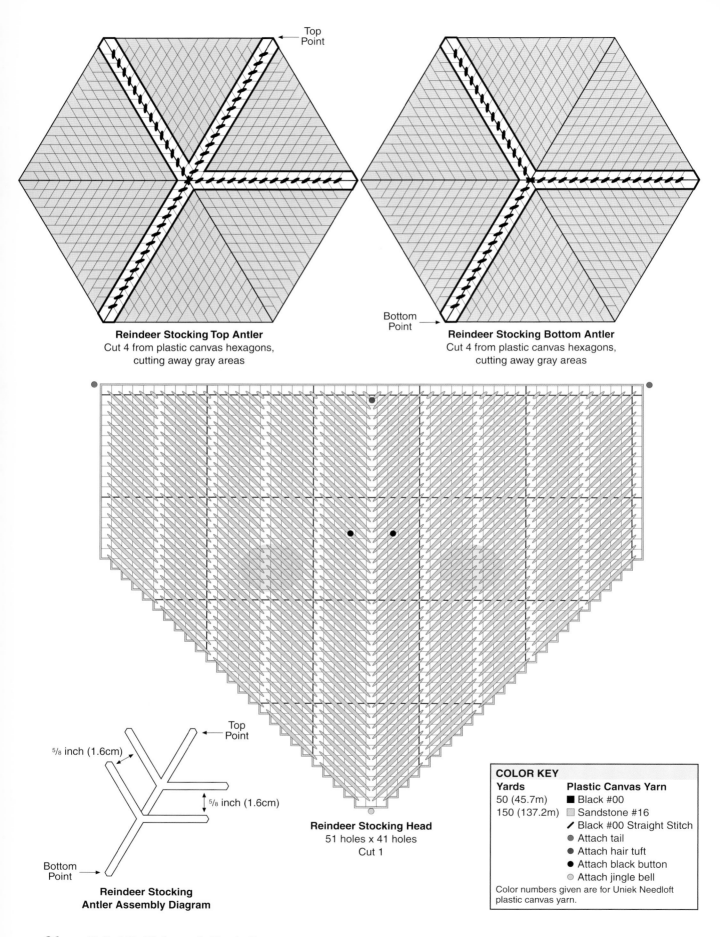

Reindeer Stocking Top Antler
Cut 4 from plastic canvas hexagons,
cutting away gray areas

Top Point

Reindeer Stocking Bottom Antler
Cut 4 from plastic canvas hexagons,
cutting away gray areas

Bottom Point

Top Point

⅝ inch (1.6cm)

⅝ inch (1.6cm)

Bottom Point

**Reindeer Stocking
Antler Assembly Diagram**

Reindeer Stocking Head
51 holes x 41 holes
Cut 1

COLOR KEY

Yards	Plastic Canvas Yarn
50 (45.7m)	■ Black #00
150 (137.2m)	☐ Sandstone #16
	╱ Black #00 Straight Stitch
	● Attach tail
	● Attach hair tuft
	● Attach black button
	○ Attach jingle bell

Color numbers given are for Uniek Needloft plastic canvas yarn.

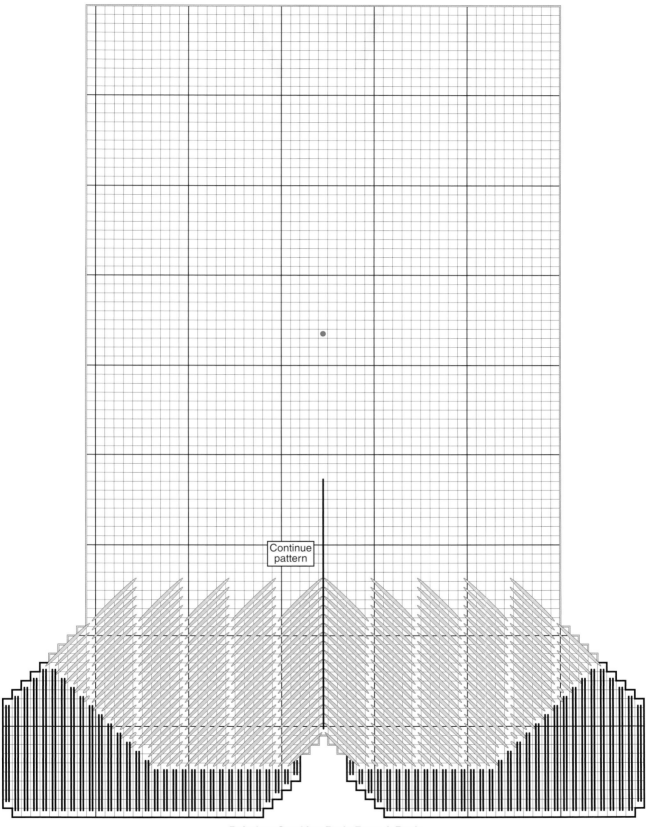

Continue
pattern

Reindeer Stocking Body Front & Back
69 holes x 90 holes
Cut 2

Plaid Pleaser

Give your next gift in style by presenting it in this handy gift bag embellished with brightly colored metallic craft cord.

DESIGN BY MARY T. COSGROVE

Skill Level
Beginner

Size
5¼ inches W x 10 inches H x 2¼ inches D (13.3cm x 25.4cm x 5.7cm)

Materials
- 1 sheet red 7-count plastic canvas
- ¼ sheet bright green 7-count plastic canvas
- Uniek Needloft plastic canvas yarn as listed in color key
- Uniek Needloft metallic craft cord as listed in color key
- #16 tapestry needle
- ½-inch (1.3cm) red 4-hole button
- Small rubber band

Instructions

1. Cut bag front from red plastic canvas and gift box from bright green plastic canvas according to graphs (page 61).

2. Cut one 34-hole x 44-hole piece for back, two 14-hole x 44-hole pieces for sides, one 34-hole x 14-hole piece for base and one 4-hole x 40-hole piece for handle from red plastic canvas. Back, sides, base and handle will remain unstitched.

3. Place bright green gift box on front piece where indicated with blue lines, then work Continental Stitches shown on gift box graph through both layers of canvas.

4. Make an eight-loop bow with 1 yard (1m) green metallic craft cord, making loops about 1½-inches (3.8cm) long. Wrap rubber band around center of bow.

5. Place bow where indicated on graph, then, using Christmas red yarn, stitch red button to bag over center of bow.

6. Using bright green yarn throughout, Whipstitch front and back to sides, then Whipstitch front, back and sides to base. Overcast top edges of bag, Whipstitching handle ends to center of sides while Overcasting. 🎄

GRAPHS ON PAGE 61

Sweet Treat Basket

Delight that special someone with a tiny treat presented in a cheerful mini basket.

DESIGN BY MARY T. COSGROVE

Skill Level
Beginner

Size
3⅝ inches H x 3⅛ inches in diameter (9.2cm x 8cm)

Materials
- 1 Uniek QuickShape 3-D plastic canvas egg
- 1 (3-inch) Uniek QuickShape plastic canvas radial circle
- Uniek Needloft plastic canvas yarn as listed in color key
- #16 tapestry needle
- Fabric glue

Instructions
1. Separate egg and cut basket side and handle according to graphs, cutting away gray areas. Cut basket base from 3-inch radial circle, cutting away gray area.
2. Stitch pieces following graphs, working red running stitches on side and handle while stitching. When background stitching is completed, work holly Straight Stitches from bottom to top, then from top to bottom around side.
3. Overcast side edges of handles with holly.
4. For bow, thread two 12-inch (30.5cm) lengths of holly yarn from back to front through top four holes of handles. Holding two tails of yarn together on each side, tie yarn in a double bow.
5. Using holly throughout, Overcast top edge of side, Whipstitching bottom edges of handle to side while Overcasting. Overcast basket base.
6. With wrong sides facing, glue base to unstitched bottom edge of basket side. 🎄

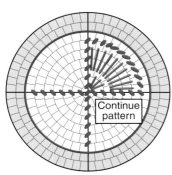

Sweet Treat Basket Base
Cut 1 from 3-inch radial circle,
cutting away gray area

COLOR KEY

Yards	Plastic Canvas Yarn
6 (6.5m)	■ Red #01
8 (7.4m)	■ Holly #27
	● Attach holly #27 bow

Color numbers given are for Uniek
Needloft plastic canvas yarn.

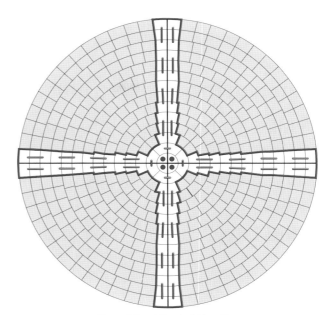

Sweet Treat Basket Handles
Cut 1 from bottom (smaller) portion of egg,
cutting away gray areas

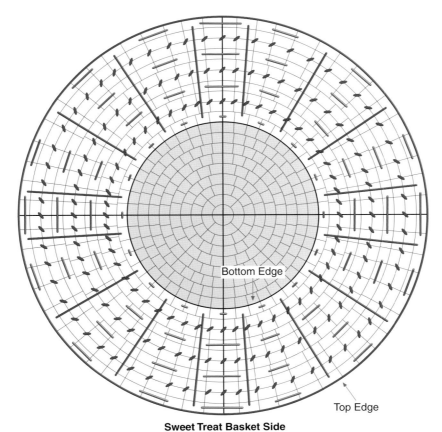

Sweet Treat Basket Side
Cut 1 from top (larger) portion of egg,
cutting away gray area

Jolly Time Mug

Although it looks like a mug, this festive gift giver is just right to fill with hot chocolate packets or holiday wrapped candies.

DESIGN BY RONDA BRYCE

Skill Level
Intermediate

Size
7¾ inches W x 5¼ inches H x 4½ inches D (19.7cm x 13.3cm x 11.4cm)

Materials
- 1 sheet 7-count plastic canvas
- 2 Uniek QuickShape 4-inch plastic canvas radial circles
- 2 Uniek QuickShape 3-inch plastic canvas radial circles
- Coats & Clark Red Heart Super Saver weight yarn Art. E300 as listed in color key
- Coats & Clark TLC Essentials weight yarn Art. E514 as listed in color key
- #16 tapestry needle
- 3 (⁷⁄₁₆-inch/1.1cm) red half-round buttons with shanks
- Hand-sewing needle
- Burgundy, green and white sewing thread

Instructions
1. Cut plastic canvas according to graphs, cutting away gray area on hot chocolate lid and marshmallow ends. Cut one 29-hole by 9-hole piece for marshmallow side. Do not cut remaining 4-inch radial circle.

2. Stitch and Overcast holly leaves and hot chocolate lid following graphs. Stitch mug and candy cane handles, reversing one handle before stitching.

3. Using white throughout, stitch marshmallow ends following graph. Continental Stitch marshmallow side, then Whipstitch short edges together, forming a circle. Whipstitch ends to side.

4. Using hand-sewing needle and white thread, stitch marshmallow to center of lid, placing marshmallow seam at bottom.

5. Using burgundy throughout, Whipstitch side edges of mug together, then Whipstitch unstitched radial circle to bottom edge. Overcast top edge.

6. Whipstitch wrong sides of handle pieces together. Using hand-sewing needle and burgundy thread, stitch handle to mug seam where indicated at brackets.

7. Using photo as a guide, and using hand-sewing needle and green thread, tack tops of holly leaves to mug. For holly berries, stitch buttons to tips of leaves and to mug using burgundy thread. ❦

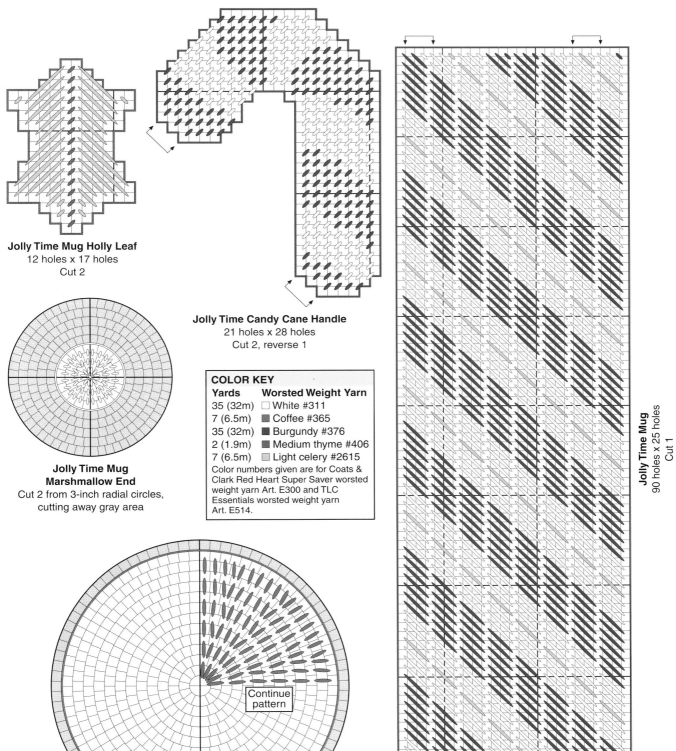

Jolly Time Mug Holly Leaf
12 holes x 17 holes
Cut 2

Jolly Time Candy Cane Handle
21 holes x 28 holes
Cut 2, reverse 1

**Jolly Time Mug
Marshmallow End**
Cut 2 from 3-inch radial circles,
cutting away gray area

COLOR KEY

Yards	Worsted Weight Yarn
35 (32m)	☐ White #311
7 (6.5m)	▨ Coffee #365
35 (32m)	■ Burgundy #376
2 (1.9m)	▨ Medium thyme #406
7 (6.5m)	▨ Light celery #2615

Color numbers given are for Coats &
Clark Red Heart Super Saver worsted
weight yarn Art. E300 and TLC
Essentials worsted weight yarn
Art. E514.

Continue
pattern

Jolly Time Mug Hot Chocolate Lid
Cut 1 from 4-inch radial circle,
cutting away gray area

Jolly Time Mug
90 holes x 25 holes
Cut 1

Warm Hands Mug

Cozy mittens add a warm loving touch to this sweet catch-all that will be a cherished gift.

DESIGN BY RONDA BRYCE

Skill Level
Intermediate

Size
6¾ inches W x 5¼ inches H x 6 inches D (17.1cm x 13.3cm x 15.2cm)

Materials
- 2 sheets 7-count plastic canvas
- 2 Uniek QuickShape 4-inch plastic canvas radial circles
- Lion Brand Yarn bulky weight yarn Article 450 as listed in color key
- Uniek Needloft plastic canvas yarn as listed in color key
- Uniek Needloft metallic craft cord as listed in color key
- #16 tapestry needle
- 4 (1-inch/25mm) white pompoms
- 9 inches (22.8cm) 2-inch/5.1cm-wide white faux fur
- Hand-sewing needle
- White and light gray sewing thread

Instructions
1. Cut plastic canvas according to graphs, cutting away gray area on hot chocolate lid. Do not cut remaining 4-inch radial circle.

2. Stitch and Overcast mittens, spoon, handle and lid following graphs, reversing one mitten before stitching.

3. Stitch mug following graph.

Using white throughout, Whipstitch side edges together, then Whipstitch unstitched radial circle to bottom edge. Overcast top edge.

4. Using hand-sewing needle and white thread through step 5, center and sew ends of handle to top and bottom edges of mug at seam.

5. Cut white faux fur in two

4½ (11.4cm) lengths. Sew one length each to cuffs of mittens where indicated in shaded yellow area, folding ends over. Part of fur will extend beyond end of mitten cuff.

6. Using photo as a guide, insert hand of left mitten through handle. Stitch tips of mittens together using hand-sewing needle and light gray thread. Wrap mittens around mug, then tack cuff ends in place with white thread.

7. Using hand-sewing needle and matching thread, securely stitch spoon handle and pompoms to center top of hot chocolate lid. 🌿

COLOR KEY

Yards	Bulky Weight Yarn
6 (5.5m)	☐ White #100
30 (27.5m)	☐ Pearl gray #150
12 (11m)	☐ Oxford gray #154
	Plastic Canvas Yarn
11 (10.1m)	☐ Cinnamon #14
40 (36.6m)	☐ White #41
	Metallic Craft Cord
7 (6.5m)	☐ Red #55003
4 (3.7m)	☐ Green #55004
1 (1m)	☐ White/silver #55008

Color numbers given are for Lion Brand Yarn Jiffy bulky weight yarn Article 450 and Uniek Needloft plastic canvas yarn and metallic craft cord.

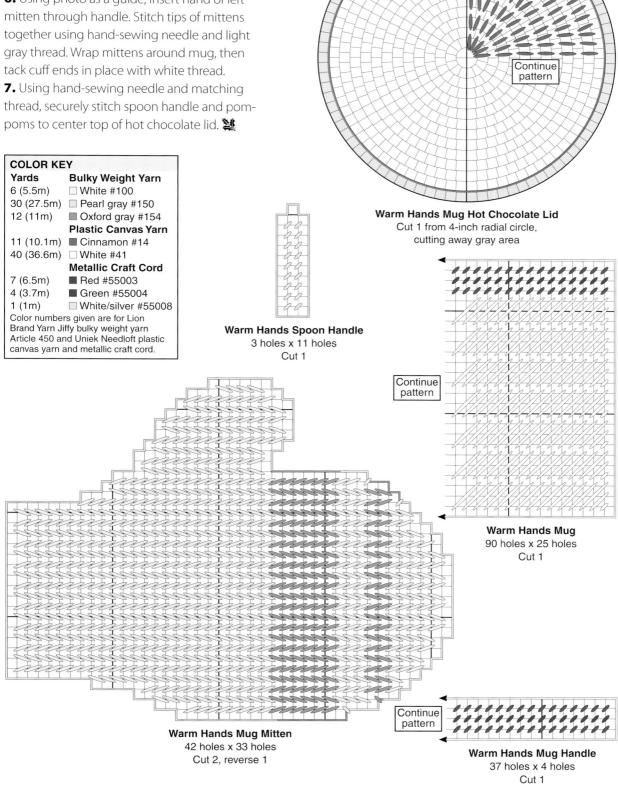

Warm Hands Mug Hot Chocolate Lid
Cut 1 from 4-inch radial circle,
cutting away gray area

Continue pattern

Warm Hands Spoon Handle
3 holes x 11 holes
Cut 1

Continue pattern

Warm Hands Mug
90 holes x 25 holes
Cut 1

Warm Hands Mug Mitten
42 holes x 33 holes
Cut 2, reverse 1

Continue pattern

Warm Hands Mug Handle
37 holes x 4 holes
Cut 1

Gift of Joy

Add some holiday glitz to an inexpensive purchased gift bag by adding a stitched plastic canvas topper.

DESIGN BY CYNTHIA ROBERTS

Skill Level
Beginner

Size
8³⁄₈ inches W x 3⁷⁄₈ inches H
(21.3cm x 9.8cm)

Materials
- 1 sheet 7-count plastic canvas
- Worsted weight yarn as listed in color key
- Metallic craft cord as listed in color key
- #16 tapestry needle
- White gift bag with handles approximately 8 x 10¹⁄₈ x 4¹⁄₄ inches (20.3cm x 25.7cm x 13.3cm)
- Craft glue

Instructions

1. Cut plastic canvas according to graphs. Back piece will remain unstitched.

2. Stitch front piece and letters following graphs. Overcast letters with silver.

3. Using blue throughout, Overcast top edges of front and back inside brackets, Whipstitch wrong sides of front and back together along remaining top edges. Overcast all remaining edges.

4. Glue letters to front following red outline given for each letter. 🍂

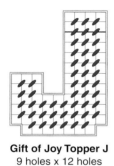

Gift of Joy Topper J
9 holes x 12 holes
Cut 1

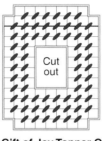

Gift of Joy Topper O
9 holes x 12 holes
Cut 1

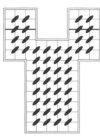

Gift of Joy Topper Y
9 holes x 12 holes
Cut 1

COLOR KEY	
Yards	**Worsted Weight Yarn**
12 (11m)	☐ White
	Metallic Craft Cord
6 (5.5m)	■ Blue
2 (1.9m)	⁄ Silver Overcast

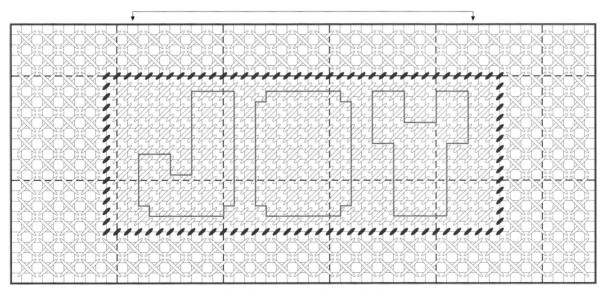

Gift of Joy Topper Front & Back
55 holes x 25 holes
Cut 2, stitch 1

Smilin' Snowman

All dressed up with his plaid scarf, this country snowman will bring a smile to your face!

DESIGN BY CYNTHIA ROBERTS

Skill Level
Beginner

Size
6⅛ inches W x 13 inches H x 2½ inches D, including handles (15.6cm x 33cm x 6.4cm)

Materials
- 2 sheets 7-count plastic canvas
- Worsted weight yarn as listed in color key
- 6-strand metallic embroidery floss as listed in color key
- #16 tapestry needle
- 12 inches (30.5cm) 1-inch/ 25mm-wide plaid ribbon
- Hot-glue gun

Instructions

1. Cut plastic canvas according to graphs (page 62), cutting out holes for scarf where indicated on front only. Cut one 40-hole x 16-hole piece for bag base. Base will remain unstitched.

2. Stitch remaining pieces following graphs, working uncoded area on white background with white Continental Stitches and uncoded areas on pale yellow background with black Continental Stitches.

3. When background stitching is completed, work black Backstitches for mouth and French Knots for eyes. Work silver metallic floss snowflakes over dark blue stitches.

4. For scarf, thread ribbon ends from back to front through cut-out holes, then tie ribbon in a knot in front, trimming ends as desired. Place a dab of glue behind scarf tails and glue to snowman.

5. Using black throughout, Overcast long edges of handles. Whipstitch front and back to sides, then Whipstitch front, back and sides to base. Overcast top edges, Whipstitching one handle to top edge of front and one to top edge of back where indicated with brackets while Overcasting.

GRAPHS ON PAGE 62

Christmas Cheer

Tiny gifts will fit perfectly in these tiny purchased gift bags dressed up with stitched toppers.

DESIGNS BY CYNTHIA ROBERTS

Skill Level
Beginner

Size
4⅞ inches W x 3⅛ inches H (12.4cm x 8cm)

Materials
- ½ sheet 7-count plastic canvas
- Worsted weight yarn as listed in color key
- Metallic craft cord as listed in color key
- #16 tapestry needle
- Christmas pin
- 1-inch (2.5cm) snowflake decoration
- 2 (½-inch/1.3cm) snowflake decorations
- 1 each brown and white small gift bags with handles approximately 4 x 5¼ x 2 inches (10.2cm x 13.3cm x 5.1cm)
- Hot-glue gun

Instructions

1. Cut topper pieces from plastic canvas according to graphs. Back pieces will remain unstitched.

2. Stitch front pieces following graphs, working uncoded area on Christmas pin topper front with black Continental Stitches and uncoded areas on snowflake topper front with turquoise Continental Stitches.

3. Using black throughout, Overcast top edges of Christmas pin topper front and back inside brackets, Whipstitch wrong sides of front and back together along remaining top edges. Overcast all remaining edges.

4. Repeat for snowflake topper pieces using turquoise.

5. Attach pin to center of Christmas pin topper front. Glue snowflakes to snowflake topper front where indicated on graph.

6. Slip Christmas pin topper over brown gift bag and snowflake topper over white bag. ✄

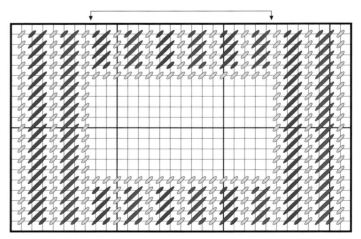

Christmas Cheer
Christmas Pin Topper Front & Back
32 holes x 20 holes
Cut 2, stitch 1

COLOR KEY

Yards	Worsted Weight Yarn
3 (2.8m)	☐ Lime green
2 (1.9m)	■ Red
2 (1.9m)	■ Green
8 (7.4m)	Uncoded areas on snowflake topper front are turquoise Continental Stitches
4 (3.7m)	Uncoded areas on Christmas pin topper front are black Continental Stitches
	⁄ Turquoise Overcast and Whipstitch
	⁄ Black Overcast and Whipstitch
Metallic Craft Cord	
4 (3.7m)	☐ Solid gold
	● Attach large snowflake
	● Attach small snowflake

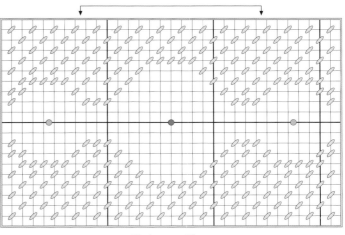

Christmas Cheer
Snowflake Topper Front & Back
32 holes x 20 holes
Cut 2, stitch 1

Mini Gift Holders

Nestle a gift card into this handy plastic canvas holder for a gift that doesn't even need to be wrapped.

DESIGNS BY BETTY HANSEN

Skill Level
Beginner

Size
3 inches W x 4⅛ inches H (7.6cm x 10.5cm)

Materials
- ½ sheet 7-count plastic canvas
- Worsted weight yarn as listed in color key
- Metallic craft cord as listed in color key
- #16 tapestry needle

Project Note
Instructions and amounts given are for one each of Santa and gift box holders.

For gift box, choose coordinating yarn and metallic craft cord colors as desired, using yarn for box color and metallic craft cord

for ribbon color. Sample gift box holders were stitched in aquas and pinks.

Instructions

1. Cut plastic canvas according to graphs.

2. Stitch and Overcast bow following graph, working Straight Stitches evenly across center part of bow.

3. Stitch remaining pieces following graphs, working uncoded background on Santa front with tan Continental Stitches and working brim of hat with two strands white yarn.

4. When background stitching is completed, work white Straight Stitches for mustache. Work French Knots, wrapping white knot three times, tan knot two times and black knots one time.

5. Overcast top edges of backs and around side and top edges on fronts from dot to dot.

6. Attach bow to gift box front where indicated with three metallic craft cord Straight Stitches over center part of bow.

7. Whipstitch wrong sides of corresponding fronts and backs together around remaining edges. ❧

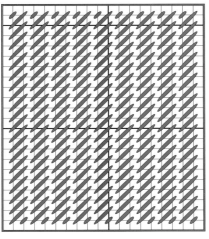

Mini Gift Holder
Santa Back
19 holes x 22 holes
Cut 1

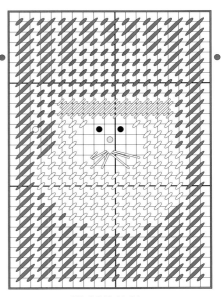

Mini Gift Holder
Santa Front
19 holes x 27 holes
Cut 1

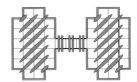

Mini Gift Holder
Gift Box Bow
11 holes x 7 holes
Cut 1

Mini Gift Holder
Gift Box Back
19 holes x 23 holes
Cut 1

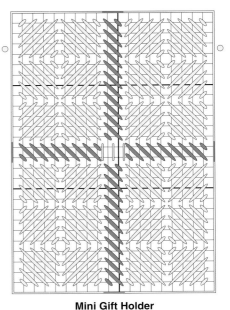

Mini Gift Holder
Gift Box Front
19 holes x 27 holes
Cut 1

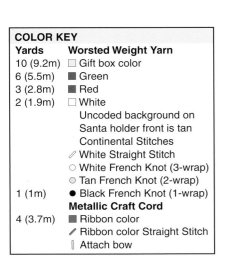

COLOR KEY

Yards	Worsted Weight Yarn
10 (9.2m)	☐ Gift box color
6 (5.5m)	◼ Green
3 (2.8m)	◼ Red
2 (1.9m)	☐ White
	Uncoded background on Santa holder front is tan Continental Stitches
	╱ White Straight Stitch
	○ White French Knot (3-wrap)
	○ Tan French Knot (2-wrap)
1 (1m)	● Black French Knot (1-wrap)
	Metallic Craft Cord
4 (3.7m)	◼ Ribbon color
	╱ Ribbon color Straight Stitch
	╎ Attach bow

Festive Fir Tree

Rich traditional Christmas colors create a striking border for the festively adorned tree featured on this tiny gift bag.

DESIGN BY ANGIE ARICKX

Skill Level
Beginner

Size
4¾ inches W x 7⅜ inches H x 2⅛ inches D (12.1cm x 18.7cm x 5.4cm)

Materials
- 1 sheet 7-count plastic canvas
- Coats & Clark Red Heart Super Saver worsted weight yarn Art. E300 as listed in color key
- Uniek Needloft plastic canvas yarn as listed in color key
- Uniek Needloft metallic craft cord as listed in color key
- #16 tapestry needle

Instructions

1. Cut and stitch plastic canvas according to graphs (this page and page 63).

2. Using white through step 3, Overcast inside edges and top edges from dot to dot on front and back. Overcast side edges of base and top and bottom edges of side panels.

3. For each side piece, Whipstitch one left panel to one right panel. Whipstitch front and back to sides and base, Overcasting bottom corners of front and back while Whipstitching.

4. Thread an 18-inch (45.7cm) length of red metallic cord through holes indicated on graph, then tie in a bow on front. 🍂

GRAPHS CONTINUED ON PAGE 63

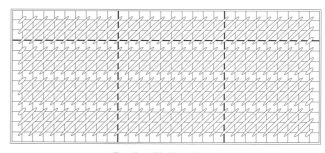

Festive Fir Tree Base
29 holes x 13 holes
Cut 1

COLOR KEY	
Yards	**Worsted Weight Yarn**
32 (29.3m)	☐ White #331
	Plastic Canvas Yarn
7 (6.5m)	◼ Christmas red #02
10 (9.2m)	◼ Holly #27
	Metallic Craft Cord
6 (5.5m)	☐ Gold #55001
1 (1m)	● Attach red #55003 bow

Color numbers given are for Coats & Clark Red Heart Super Saver worsted weight yarn Art. E300 and Uniek Needloft plastic canvas yarn and metallic craft cord.

Jolly Snowman Canister

Stylish and cute, this snowman is complete with fringy earmuffs and scarf. Doubling as a canister, this project is perfect for giving a gift of homemade cookies.

DESIGN BY DEBRA ARCH

Skill Level
Intermediate

Size
8 inches H x 7 inches in diameter (20.3cm x 17.8cm)

With earmuffs: 9¼ inches W (24.1cm)

Materials
- 1 artist-size sheet 7-count plastic canvas
- 1 (3-inch) Uniek QuickShape 3-D globe
- 1 (9-inch) Uniek QuickShape plastic canvas radial circles
- 2 (6-inch) Uniek QuickShape plastic canvas radial circles
- 1 (6-inch) Uniek QuickShape plastic canvas heart
- Coats & Clark Red Heart Plush worsted weight yarn Art. E719 as listed in color key
- Lion Brand Yarn Fun Fur bulky weight eyelash yarn Article 320 as listed in color key
- Kreinik ⅛-inch Ribbon as listed in color key
- #16 tapestry needle
- 2 (¾-inch/1.9cm) black shank buttons
- 7 (⁷⁄₁₆-inch/1.1cm) black half-round buttons
- 34.5 ounce empty clean coffee can
- Peach blush
- Cotton swab
- Old clean toothbrush
- White spray paint (optional)
- Shank cutter (optional)
- Hot-glue gun

Cutting & Stitching

1. Cut plastic canvas according to graphs (pages 58, 59 and 60), cutting away gray areas on ear muffs and head rim (9-inch plastic canvas circle) and on lid handles (plastic canvas heart).

2. Cut one 105-hole x 4-hole piece for lid lip. Cut away 16 innermost rows of holes from one 6-inch radial circle for lid liner, leaving the three outermost rows of holes. Lid lip and lid liner will remain unstitched.

3. Stitch pieces following graphs using 2 strands white for head and lid, 1 strand each bright blue and lime for scarf, 2 strands lime for earmuffs and 2 strands chartreuse for headband, stitching both halves of globe for earmuffs.

Assembly

1. Use photo as a guide throughout assembly. Whipstitch side edges of head together with adjacent colors, forming back seam. Using white, Whipstitch outside edge of head rim to top edge of head; Overcast inside edge of rim.

2. Overcast earmuffs and headband. Glue headband to center front at top, then glue earmuffs to head at ends of headband.

3. Overcast nose and glue in place where indicated on graph with peach shading. Use a cotton swab to apply blush where indicated with pink shading.

4. If desired, cut shanks from buttons. Glue large buttons to head for eyes and smaller buttons to head for mouth where indicated on graph.

5. Using white through step 6, Whipstitch wrong sides of lid handle together, then stitch handle to center top of lid.

6. Whipstitch short edges of lid lip together forming a circle, then Whipstitch lip to inside edges of lid liner. Place liner on wrong side of lid, then Whipstitch around outside edge.

7. Use toothbrush to brush up nap of eyelash yarn on scarf and earmuffs to create a furry effect.

8. If desired, spray coffee can with white spray paint. Allow to dry. Slide snowman head down over can.

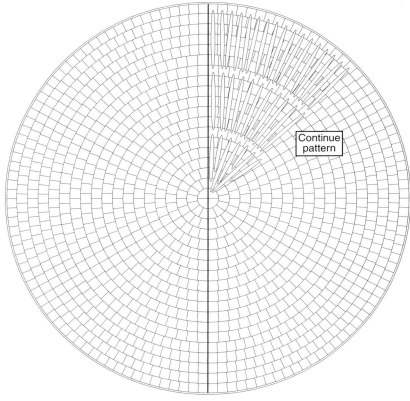

Jolly Snowman Canister Lid
Stitch 1 (6-inch) radial circle

Jolly Snowman Canister Nose
10 holes x 4 holes
Cut 1

**Jolly Snowman Canister
Lid Handles**
Cut 2 from plastic canvas heart,
cutting away gray area

COLOR KEY

Yards	Worsted Weight Yarn
170 (155.5m)	☐ White #9001 (2 strands)
	Bulky Weight Eyelash Yarn
30 (27.5m)	☐ Bright blue #106 (1 strand) and
80 (73.2m)	lime #194 (1 strand) combined
	☐ Lime #194 (2 strands)
	1/8-inch Ribbon
25 (22.9m)	☐ Chartreuse #015
2 (1.9m)	☐ Light peach #9192
	○ Attach large button
	● Attach small button

Color numbers given are for Coats & Clark Red Heart Plush worsted weight yarn Art. E719, Lion Brand Yarn Fun Fur bulky weight eyelash yarn Article 320 and Kreinik 1/8-inch Ribbon.

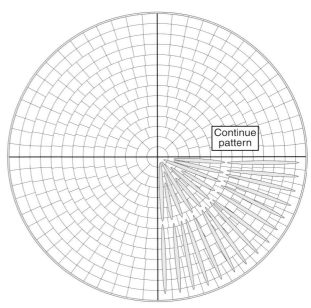

Jolly Snowman Canister Earmuff
Stitch both halves of globe

Jolly Snowman Canister Earmuffs Headband
Cut 1 from 9-inch radial circle, cutting away gray areas

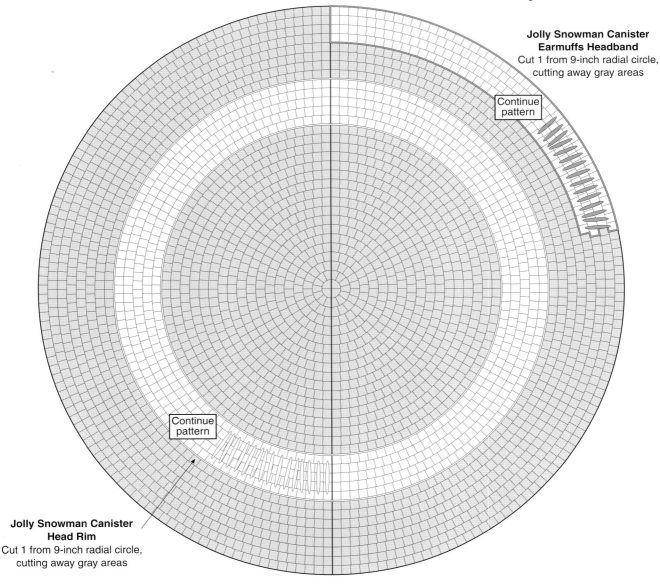

Jolly Snowman Canister Head Rim
Cut 1 from 9-inch radial circle, cutting away gray areas

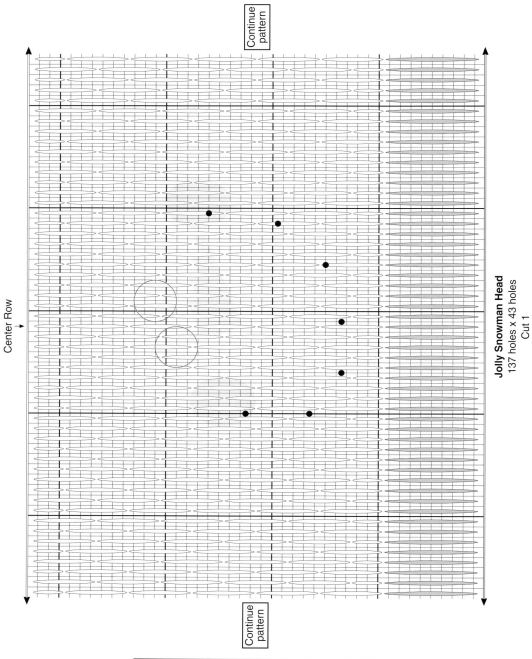

Continue pattern

Continue pattern

Center Row

Jolly Snowman Head
137 holes x 43 holes
Cut 1

COLOR KEY	
Yards	**Worsted Weight Yarn**
170 (155.5m)	☐ White #9001 (2 strands)
	Bulky Weight Eyelash Yarn
30 (27.5m)	◻ Bright blue #106 (1 strand) and
80 (73.2m)	lime #194 (1 strand) combined
	☐ Lime #194 (2 strands)
	¹/₈-inch Ribbon
25 (22.9m)	◼ Chartreuse #015
2 (1.9m)	☐ Light peach #9192
	○ Attach large button
	● Attach small button

Color numbers given are for Coats & Clark Red Heart Plush worsted weight yarn Art. E719, Lion Brand Yarn Fun Fur bulky weight eyelash yarn Article 320 and Kreinik ¹/₈-inch Ribbon.

Plaid Pleaser

CONTINUED FROM PAGE 38

COLOR KEY

Yards	Plastic Canvas Yarn
2 (1.9m)	■ Christmas red #01
5 (4.6m)	⁄ Bright green #61 Overcast and Whipstitch
	Metallic Craft Cord
4 (3.7m)	■ Green #55004
	❙ Attach button and bow

Color numbers given are for Uniek Needloft plastic canvas yarn and metallic craft cord.

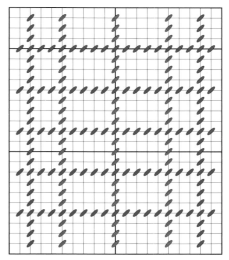

Plaid Pleaser Gift Box
20 holes x 24 holes
Cut 1 from bright green

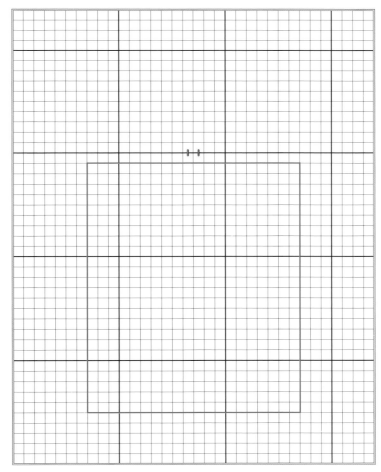

Plaid Pleaser Front
34 holes x 44 holes
Cut 1 from Christmas red

Smilin' Snowman

CONTINUED FROM PAGE 48

Smilin' Snowman Front & Back
40 holes x 52 holes
Cut 2,
cutting out holes on front only

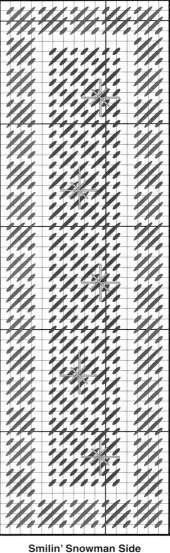

Smilin' Snowman Side
16 holes x 52 holes
Cut 2

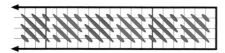

Smilin' Snowman Handle
76 holes x 4 holes
Cut 2

COLOR KEY	
Yards	**Worsted Weight Yarn**
18 (16.5m)	■ Dark blue
14 (12.9m)	■ Green
12 (11m)	■ Red
1 (1m)	■ Orange
20 (18.3m)	Uncoded areas on white background are white Continental Stitches
20 (18.3m)	Uncoded areas on pale yellow background are black Continental Stitches
	╱ Black Backstitch, Overcast and Whipstitch
	● Black French Knot
	6-Strand Metallic Embroidery Floss
9 (8.3m)	╱ Silver Straight Stitch

Festive Fir Tree

CONTINUED FROM PAGE 54

Festive Fir Tree Side Panel
7 holes x 36 holes
Cut 4
Stitch 2 as graphed
for side right panels
Reverse 2 for side left panels
and work stitching in reverse

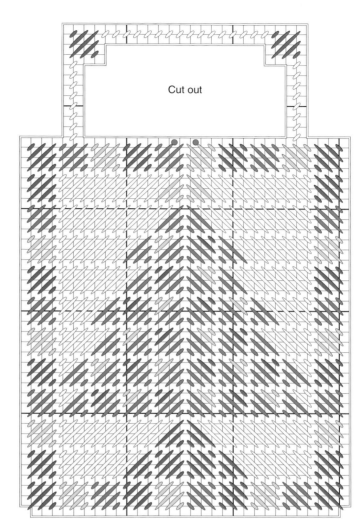

Cut out

Festive Fir Tree Bag Front & Back
31 holes x 48 holes
Cut 2

COLOR KEY		
Yards	**Worsted Weight Yarn**	
32 (29.3m)	□ White #331	
	Plastic Canvas Yarn	
7 (6.5m)	■ Christmas red #02	
10 (9.2m)	■ Holly #27	
	Metallic Craft Cord	
6 (5.5m)	▨ Gold #55001	
1 (1m)	● Attach red #55003 bow	

Color numbers given are for Coats & Clark Red Heart Super Saver worsted weight yarn Art. E300 and Uniek Needloft plastic canvas yarn and metallic craft cord.

Festive Ornaments

Trim the tree with ornaments ranging from elegant to whimsical. Whatever your holiday decorating style, you'll love stitching these festive designs.

Sweet Treat Pals

Cute as ornaments or as tiny gifts, these darling pals will hold a pack of gum, candy or mints for a sweet holiday treat!

DESIGNS BY JUDY COLLISHAW

Skill Level
Beginner

Size
Angel: 5 inches W x 5 inches H (12.7cm x 12.7cm)

Cat: 3⅞ inches W x 5⅜ inches H (9.8cm x 13.7cm)

Dog: 3⅜ inches x 4¼ inches H (8.6cm x 10.8cm)

Penguin: 3 inches x 6¼ inches H (7.6cm x 15.9cm)

Santa: 3¼ inches x 5⅝ inches H (8.3cm x 14.3cm)

Snowman: 3⅜ inches x 5¾ inches H (8.6cm x 14.6cm)

Materials
Each
- ½ sheet 7-count plastic canvas
- Worsted weight yarn as listed in color key
- #5 pearl cotton as listed in color key, excluding penguin
- #16 tapestry needle
- 2½-inch/6.4cm-length ¼-inch/6mm-wide white braided elastic
- Hand-sewing needle
- White sewing thread
- 6 inches (16.2cm) thin gold thread
- Hot-glue gun

Angel
- Uniek Needloft metallic craft cord as listed in color key
- 2 (4mm) black beads
- Black sewing thread

Cat
- 2 (5mm) black beads
- Black sewing thread

Dog
- 6mm black cabochon
- 6 inches (16.2cm) ⅛-inch/ 3mm-wide polka dot satin ribbon

Penguin
- ³⁄₁₆-inch (5mm) white pompom
- 2 (4mm) black beads
- Black sewing thread

Santa
- ½-inch (12mm) white pompom
- 2 (4mm) black beads
- Black sewing thread

Snowman
- ⅝-inch (1.6cm) white snowflake button
- 2 (4mm) black beads
- Black sewing thread

Cutting & Stitching
1. Cut plastic canvas according to graphs (pages 69, 70 and 71).

2. Overcast Santa mustache with white. Stitch pieces following graphs, working uncoded areas with Continental Stitches as follows: angel and Santa pieces with peach, cat pieces with light gray, dog pieces with medium rust, penguin pieces with burgundy, snowman pieces with white.

3. Overcast all pieces, leaving edges inside brackets on bodies, arms, forelegs and flippers unworked at this time.

Angel
1. Work pale yellow Turkey Loop Stitches where indicated with yellow shading, making loops approximately ¼-inch/0.6cm-long.

2. Work red yarn French Knots on arms and body. Work red pearl cotton Fly Stitch for mouth. Using hand-sewing needle and black sewing thread, attach beads to head for eyes where indicated.

3. Overlap ends of braided elastic approximately ¼-inch (0.6cm), forming a loop. **Note:** *This loop must fit snugly around candy, mints or gum, so adjust as necessary before stitching.* Use a double strand white sewing thread to securely stitch overlapped edges on both

sides. Glue overlapped section of loop to center back of hands.

4. Using white, Whipstitch arms to body where indicated with brackets.

5. Using photo as a guide through step 6, cut a 3-inch/7.6cm-length gold metallic craft cord. Glue ends together, forming a halo, then glue halo to head.

6. Glue head to top of body at a slight angle; glue wings to back of body.

7. For hanger, tie ends of 6-inch/16.2cm length of thin gold thread together in a knot to form a loop for hanging. Glue knot to back of head where indicated with an arrow.

8. Insert gum, candy or mints through elastic loop.

Cat

1. Work green French Knots on scarf, wrapping needle one time. Work rose French Knot nose, wrapping needle three times.

2. Work pink pearl cotton Backstitches for mouth. Using hand-sewing needle and black sewing thread, attach beads to head for eyes where indicated.

3. Following steps 3 and 4 for angel, attach loop to forelegs, then attach forelegs to body with light gray.

4. Using photo as guide, glue head to body at a slight angle. Attach hanger to head following step 7 of angel instructions.

5. Insert gum, candy or mints through elastic loop.

Dog

1. Work black yarn Straight Stitches for eyes and black pearl cotton Backstitches for mouth.

2. Glue cabochon to head for nose where indicated on graph. Tie polka dot ribbon in a bow and glue to head where indicated.

3. Following steps 3 and 4 for angel, attach loop to forelegs, then attach forelegs to body with dark brown.

4. Using photo as guide, glue head to body at a slight angle. Attach hanger to head following step 7 of angel instructions.

5. Insert gum, candy or mints through elastic loop.

Penguin

1. Work yellow Straight Stitches on head for beak. Using hand-sewing needle and black sewing thread, attach beads to head for eyes where indicated.

2. Following steps 3 and 4 for angel, attach loop to flippers, then attach flippers to body with black.

3. Glue pompom to top of hat where indicated on graph. Glue hat to head and head to top of body at a slight angle. Glue feet to bottom of body. Attach hanger to head following step 7 of angel instructions.

4. Insert gum, candy or mints through elastic loop.

Santa

1. Work rose French Knot for nose wrapping needle three times. Work light steel gray pearl cotton Backstitches to separate hands and feet.

2. Using hand-sewing needle and black sewing thread, attach beads to head for eyes where indicated.

3. Following steps 3 and 4 for angel, attach loop to arms, then attach arms to body with red.

4. Using photo as guide, glue mustache to head between mouth and nose, glue pompom to tip of hat where indicated on graph. Glue head to body. Attach hanger to head following step 7 of angel instructions.

5. Insert gum, candy or mints through elastic loop.

Snowman

1. Work orange Straight Stitches for nose. Using pearl cotton, work black Backstitches for mouth and light steel gray pearl cotton Backstitches to separate hands and feet.

2. Using hand-sewing needle and black sewing thread, attach beads to head for eyes where indicated. Use white thread to attach snowflake button to hat where indicated.

3. Following steps 3 and 4 for angel, attach loop to arms, then attach arms to body with white.

4. Using photo as guide, glue hat to head at a slight angle, then glue head to body at a slight angle. Attach hanger to hat following step 7 of angel instructions.

5. Insert gum, candy or mints through elastic loop. 🦋

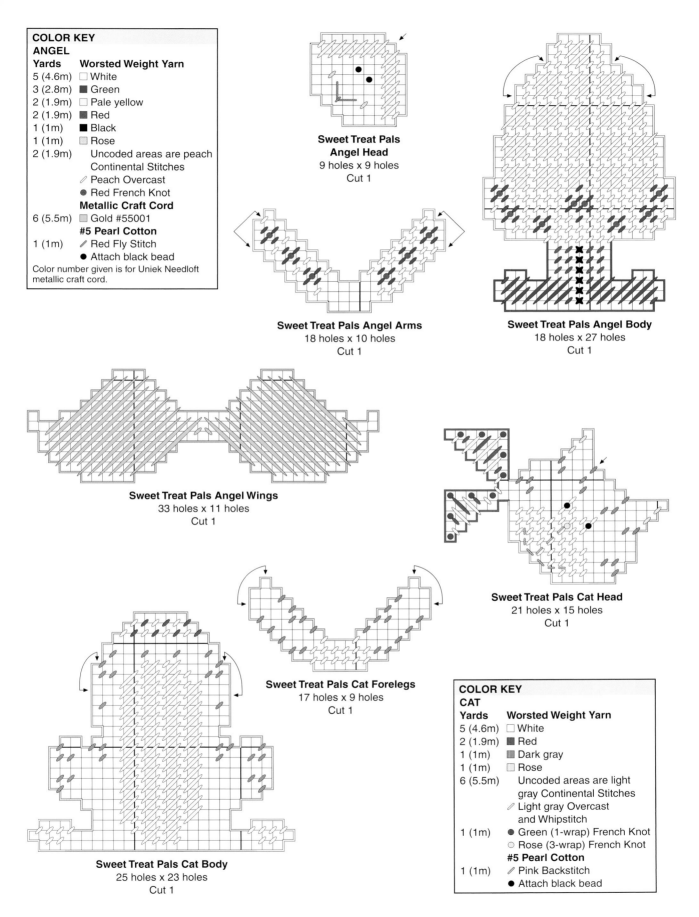

COLOR KEY
ANGEL

Yards	Worsted Weight Yarn
5 (4.6m)	☐ White
3 (2.8m)	■ Green
2 (1.9m)	☐ Pale yellow
2 (1.9m)	■ Red
1 (1m)	■ Black
1 (1m)	☐ Rose
2 (1.9m)	Uncoded areas are peach Continental Stitches
	╱ Peach Overcast
	● Red French Knot
	Metallic Craft Cord
6 (5.5m)	☐ Gold #55001
	#5 Pearl Cotton
1 (1m)	╱ Red Fly Stitch
	● Attach black bead

Color number given is for Uniek Needloft metallic craft cord.

Sweet Treat Pals Angel Head
9 holes x 9 holes
Cut 1

Sweet Treat Pals Angel Arms
18 holes x 10 holes
Cut 1

Sweet Treat Pals Angel Body
18 holes x 27 holes
Cut 1

Sweet Treat Pals Angel Wings
33 holes x 11 holes
Cut 1

Sweet Treat Pals Cat Head
21 holes x 15 holes
Cut 1

Sweet Treat Pals Cat Forelegs
17 holes x 9 holes
Cut 1

Sweet Treat Pals Cat Body
25 holes x 23 holes
Cut 1

COLOR KEY
CAT

Yards	Worsted Weight Yarn
5 (4.6m)	☐ White
2 (1.9m)	■ Red
1 (1m)	■ Dark gray
1 (1m)	☐ Rose
6 (5.5m)	Uncoded areas are light gray Continental Stitches
	╱ Light gray Overcast and Whipstitch
1 (1m)	● Green (1-wrap) French Knot
	○ Rose (3-wrap) French Knot
	#5 Pearl Cotton
1 (1m)	╱ Pink Backstitch
	● Attach black bead

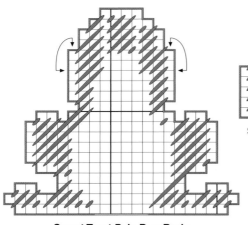

Sweet Treat Pals Dog Body
22 holes x 20 holes
Cut 1

Sweet Treat Pals Dog Head
14 holes x 10 holes
Cut 1

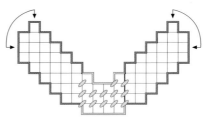

Sweet Treat Pals Dog Forelegs
16 holes x 9 holes
Cut 1

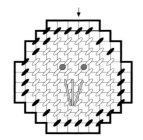

Sweet Treat Pals Penguin Head
11 holes x 11 holes
Cut 1

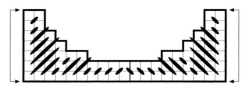

Sweet Treat Pals Penguin Flippers
19 holes x 7 holes
Cut 1

COLOR KEY	
DOG	
Yards	**Worsted Weight Yarn**
7 (6.5m)	▨ Dark brown
1 (1m)	▨ Tan
1 (1m)	■ Black
3 (2.8m)	Uncoded areas are medium rust Continental Stitches
	╱ Medium rust Overcast
	╱ Black Straight Stitch
#5 Pearl Cotton	
1 (1m)	╱ Black Backstitch
	● Attach black cabochon
	● Attach ribbon bow

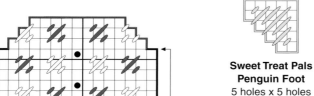

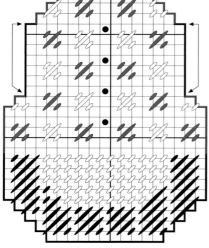

Sweet Treat Pals Penguin Body
19 holes x 24 holes
Cut 1

Sweet Treat Pals Penguin Foot
5 holes x 5 holes
Cut 2

Sweet Treat Pals Penguin Hat
7 holes x 5 holes
Cut 1

COLOR KEY	
PENGUIN	
Yards	**Worsted Weight Yarn**
5 (4.6m)	■ Black
3 (2.8m)	□ White
2 (1.9m)	▨ Yellow
1 (1m)	▨ Green
3 (2.8m)	Uncoded areas are burgundy Continental Stitches
	╱ Burgundy Overcast
	╱ Yellow Straight Stitch
	● Black French Knot
	● Attach black bead
	○ Attach white pompom

COLOR KEY
SANTA
Yards	Worsted Weight Yarn
6 (5.5m)	■ Red
2 (1.9m)	■ Burgundy
2 (1.9m)	■ Black
2 (1.9m)	□ Cream
2 (1.9m)	□ White
1 (1m)	□ Rose
1 (1m)	□ Yellow
1 (1m)	Uncoded areas are peach Continental Stitches
	○ Rose (3-wrap) French Knot
	#5 Pearl Cotton
1 (1m)	╱ Light steel gray Backstitch
	● Attach black bead
	○ Attach white pompom

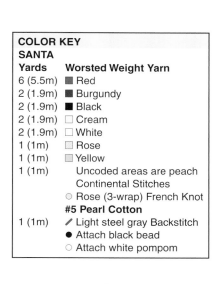

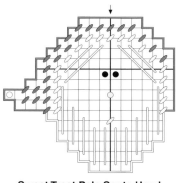

Sweet Treat Pals Santa Head
16 holes x 15 holes
Cut 1

Sweet Treat Pals Santa Mustache
5 holes x 2 holes
Cut 1

Sweet Treat Pals Santa Arms
21 holes x 9 holes
Cut 1

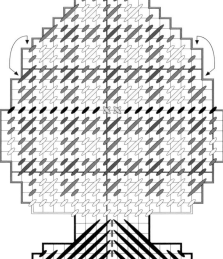

Sweet Treat Pals Santa Body
21 holes x 28 holes
Cut 1

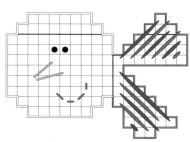

Sweet Treat Pals Snowman Head
17 holes x 12 holes
Cut 1

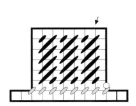

Sweet Treat Pals Snowman Arms
19 holes x 10 holes
Cut 1

COLOR KEY
SNOWMAN
Yards	Worsted Weight Yarn
8 (7.4m)	□ White
3 (2.8m)	■ Red
2 (1.9m)	■ Black
1 (1m)	■ Green
1 (1m)	□ Yellow
	Uncoded areas are white Continental Stitches
1 (1m)	╱ Orange Straight Stitch
	#5 Pearl Cotton
1 (1m)	╱ Black Backstitch
1 (1m)	╱ Light steel gray Backstitch
	● Attach black bead
	○ Attach snowflake

Sweet Treat Pals Snowman Hat
11 holes x 7 holes
Cut 1

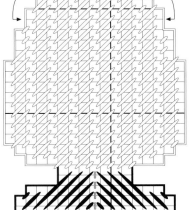

Sweet Treat Pals Snowman Body
17 holes x 24 holes
Cut 1

Santa's Helper

Dressed up with a bow and jingle bell, this reindeer is ready for Christmas. Hang this ornament on your tree or stand on your mantel for holiday cheer.

DESIGN BY DEBORAH SCHEBLEIN

Skill Level
Beginner

Size
4½ inches L x 6¾ inches H x 2¾ inches D (11.4cm x 17.1cm x 7cm)

Materials
- 1 sheet 7-count plastic canvas
- Worsted weight yarn as listed in color key
- #16 tapestry needle
- ⅜-inch (1cm) gold jingle bell, optional
- 18 inches (45.7cm) ⅛-inch/ 3mm-wide red satin ribbon
- Hot-glue gun

Cutting & Stitching

1. Cut plastic canvas according to graphs.

2. Following graphs throughout, stitching one body as graphed. Reverse remaining body and work stitches in reverse.

3. When background stitching is completed, work French Knots for eyes with dark brown.

4. Stitch ears/antlers front following graph. Stitch blue shaded areas on back of ears replacing off-white with golden brown.

5. Stitch tail front following graph. Stitch tail back replacing golden brown with off-white.

Assembly

1. Whipstitch wrong sides of the following together: body pieces, two sets of legs, tail pieces and ear/antler pieces.

2. Insert body in legs, tail and ears/antlers where indicated on graph; glue in place.

3. Cut ribbon in one 6-inch/15.2cm length and one 12-inch/30.5cm length.

4. If using jingle bell, thread it onto 6-inch/15.2cm length and tie around neck. Using photo as a guide, place bow at side of neck. Jingle bell can hang below neck.

5. For hanger, thread 12-inch/30.5cm length through holes indicated on body. Tie ends together in a knot to form a loop for hanging. 🍃

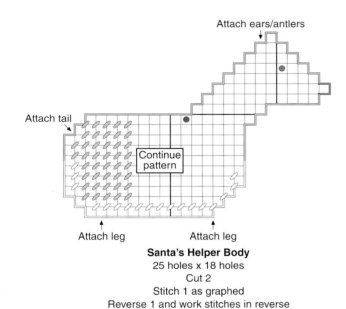

Attach ears/antlers

Attach tail

Continue pattern

Attach leg   Attach leg

Santa's Helper Body
25 holes x 18 holes
Cut 2
Stitch 1 as graphed
Reverse 1 and work stitches in reverse

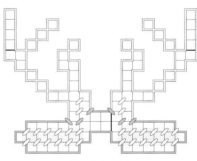

**Santa's Helper
Ears/Antlers Front & Back**
18 holes x 14 holes
Cut 2
Stitch front as graphed
Stitch back replacing off-white in
blue shaded area with golden brown

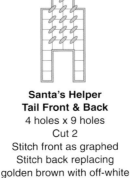

**Santa's Helper
Tail Front & Back**
4 holes x 9 holes
Cut 2
Stitch front as graphed
Stitch back replacing
golden brown with off-white

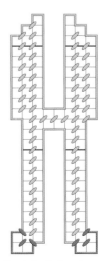

Santa's Helper Legs
8 holes x 23 holes
Cut 4

COLOR KEY

Yards	Worsted Weight Yarn
15 (13.8m)	▨ Golden brown
4 (3.7m)	☐ Off-white
1 (1m)	▩ Dark brown
	● Dark brown French Knot
	● Attach hanging ribbon

Belle

Dressed to the nines in a brimmed hat, mittens and plaid scarf, this snow "woman" ornament also doubles as a bell.

DESIGN BY LEE LINDEMAN

Skill Level
Beginner

Size
3¾ inches W x 6¼ inches H
(9.5cm x 15.9cm)

Materials
- 1 sheet 7-count plastic canvas
- Uniek Needloft plastic canvas yarn as listed in color key
- 6-strand embroidery floss as listed in color key
- #16 tapestry needle
- 2 (5mm) black cabochons
- 3 (6mm) black cabochons
- Small amount black craft foam
- 6 inches (15.2cm) ¼-inch/7mm-wide red satin ribbon
- 8 inches (20.3cm) ½-inch/12mm-wide red gingham ribbon for scarf
- 2 (¾-inch/19mm) jingle bells
- Small amount orange polymer clay
- Small amount fiberfill
- Hot-glue gun

Cutting & Stitching

1. Cut plastic canvas according to graphs (this page and page 76), cutting out small hole in center of gusset.

2. Using pattern given (page 76), cut one hat brim from black craft foam, cutting out center hole.

3. Stitch and Overcast arms and pocket following graphs, reversing one arm before stitching.

4. Stitch remaining pieces following graphs, leaving tabs on head pieces unstitched as indicated.

5. When background stitching is completed, use 2 plies black floss to work Backstitches on head front only.

Assembly

1. Using white through step 4, Overcast inside edges of gusset.

Whipstitch one long edge of gusset around side and top of body front, easing as necessary to fit.

2. Whipstitch wrong sides of head pieces together, filling with a small amount of fiberfill before closing.

3. Insert tab on head in opening of gusset; glue to secure. To attach jingle bells, thread a 2½–3 inch (6.4–7.6cm) length of yarn through hole indicated on tab. Attach ends to bells.

4. Whipstitch body back to gusset, easing as necessary to fit. Overcast bottom edges of front, back and gusset.

5. Using photo as a guide through step 9, glue arms to gusset, making sure thumbs are up. Glue pocket to front where indicated with red lines.

6. Glue 6mm black cabochons to body front for buttons. Glue 5mm black cabochons to head for eyes.

7. Following manufacturer's instructions, make ⅝-inch/ 1.6cm-long pointed nose from orange polymer clay. Glue to face where indicated.

8. Slide hat brim over head and glue in place where black and white stitches meet. Wrap red satin ribbon around head just above rim, crisscrossing ends in back; glue in place.

9. Tie ribbon for scarf around neck, knotting at side. Glue tails to front and back. 🌿

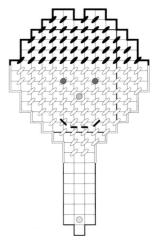

Belle Head Front & Back
13 holes x 22 holes
Cut 2
Work Backstitches on front only

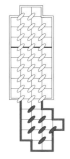

Belle Arm
5 holes x 14 holes
Cut 2, reverse 1

Belle Pocket
5 holes x 5 holes
Cut 1

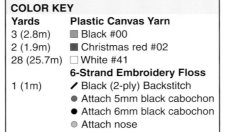

COLOR KEY		
Yards	**Plastic Canvas Yarn**	
3 (2.8m)	■ Black #00	
2 (1.9m)	■ Christmas red #02	
28 (25.7m)	□ White #41	
	6-Strand Embroidery Floss	
1 (1m)	╱ Black (2-ply) Backstitch	
	● Attach 5mm black cabochon	
	● Attach 6mm black cabochon	
	○ Attach nose	
	○ Attach jingle bells	

Color numbers given are for Uniek Needloft plastic canvas yarn.

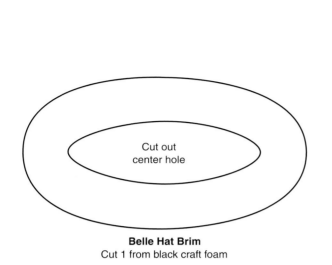

Belle Hat Brim
Cut 1 from black craft foam

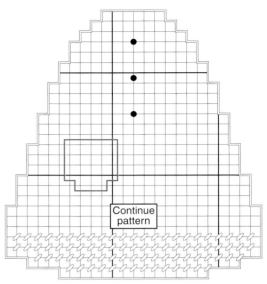

Continue pattern

Belle Body Front & Back
24 holes x 26 holes
Cut 2

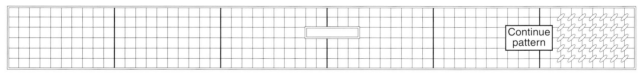

Continue pattern

Belle Gusset
59 holes x 6 holes
Cut 1

COLOR KEY	
Yards	**Plastic Canvas Yarn**
3 (2.8m)	▨ Black #00
2 (1.9m)	◼ Christmas red #02
28 (25.7m)	☐ White #41
	6-Strand Embroidery Floss
1 (1m)	╱ Black (2-ply) Backstitch
	● Attach 5mm black cabochon
	● Attach 6mm black cabochon
	○ Attach nose
	○ Attach jingle bells

Color numbers given are for Uniek Needloft plastic canvas yarn.

Angel Elegance

Iridescent craft cord adds sparkle and elegance to this gorgeous ornament that surrounds a tiny angel.

DESIGN BY ANGIE ARICKX

Skill Level
Intermediate

Size
4⅛ inches H x 3½ inches in diameter, excluding hanger (10.5cm x 8.9cm)

Materials
- ¼ sheet 7-count plastic canvas
- 2 (5-inch) Uniek QuickShape plastic canvas hearts
- Uniek Needloft plastic canvas yarn as listed in color key
- #16 tapestry needle
- Miniature angel ornament
- Hanging filament as desired
- Hot-glue gun

Instructions
1. Cut plastic canvas according to graphs (page 94), cutting away gray areas on stars (globe sections).
2. Following graphs throughout, stitch and Overcast snowflakes. Stitch globe sections, overlapping shaded blue corners before stitching, forming a globe.
3. Overcast globe edges with white iridescent cord.
4. Hang angel inside globe, threading hanging filament though top

hole of globe where indicated on graph and securing on top.
5. For globe hanger, thread desired length of white iridescent cord from back to front through one snowflake where indicated on graph. Tie ends together in a knot

to form a loop for hanging. Glue this snowflake to globe top.
6. Glue one snowflake to globe bottom and remaining five snowflakes on overlapped corners. ❧

GRAPHS ON PAGE 94

Christmas Cardinal

Rich red chenille yarn mimics the look of feathers on this handsome cardinal ornament featuring a jingle bell!

DESIGN BY DEBRA ARCH

Skill Level
Intermediate

Size
5⅝ inches L x 4⅞ inches H x 1½ inches D (14.3cm x 12.4cm x 3.8cm)

Materials
- ½ sheet 7-count plastic canvas
- 2 (5-inch) Uniek QuickShape plastic canvas hexagons
- Coats & Clark Red Heart Plush worsted weight yarn Art E719 as listed in color key
- Uniek Needloft plastic canvas yarn as listed in color key
- #16 tapestry needle
- 2½ yards (2.3m) ⅜-inch/9mm-wide gold decorative ribbon
- 1 inch (25mm) gold jingle bell
- 2 (3-inch/7.6m) lengths 26-gauge gold wire
- 2 (6mm) gold faceted beads
- Long doll needle
- Hot-glue gun

Instructions

1. Cut plastic canvas according to graphs, cutting away gray areas on gussets (hexagons).

2. Stitch pieces following graphs, reversing one body and one wing before stitching. Overcast wings.

3. Whipstitch body pieces together from beak, around top of head and body to tip of tail from blue dot to blue dot.

4. Whipstitch long edges of base to bottom edges of tail and front gussets, forming one long strip. Whipstitch gusset strip to bottom of body.

5. Thread an 18-inch/45.7cm length of ribbon through doll needle. Insert needle into center top of body where indicated with arrow. Bring needle through body, exiting at center of base. Thread jingle bell on ribbon then bring needle back up through base and body and out through same hole at top. Tie ends together in a knot to form a loop for hanging.

6. Using photo as a guide through step 7, glue wings to body. Glue beads to head for eyes where indicated on graph.

7. Cut remaining ribbon in half. Form each half in a multiloop bow, securing each with gold wire. Glue bows to base where indicated on graph. 🪶

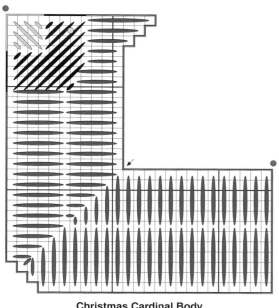

Christmas Cardinal Body
25 holes x 27 holes
Cut 2, reverse 1

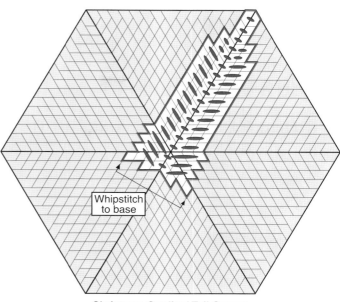

Christmas Cardinal Tail Gusset
Cut 1 from plastic canvas hexagon,
cutting away gray area

Whipstitch to front gusset

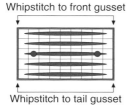

Whipstitch to tail gusset

Christmas Cardinal Base
9 holes x 5 holes
Cut 1

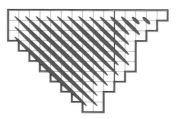

Christmas Cardinal Wing
15 holes x 10 holes
Cut 2, reverse 1

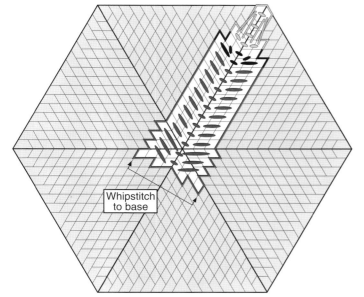

Christmas Cardinal Front Gusset
Cut 1 from plastic canvas hexagon,
cutting away gray area

COLOR KEY		
Yards	**Worsted Weight Yarn**	
50 (45.7m)	■ Red #9907	
	Plastic Canvas Yarn	
3 (2.8m)	■ Black #00	
3 (2.8m)	▨ Tangerine #11	
	⁄ Tangerine #11 Straight Stitch	
	○ Attach gold bead	
	● Attach multiloop bow	

Color numbers given are for Coats & Clark Red
Heart Plush worsted weight yarn Art. #E719 and
Uniek Needloft plastic canvas yarn.

Buddy Bears

Add a loving touch to your tree with these tiny bears nestled inside a plastic canvas chimney and heart.

DESIGNS BY ANGIE ARICKX

Skill Level
Beginner

Size
Chimney Bear: 2¼ inches W x 2⅞ inches H x 1 inch D, excluding hanger (5.7cm x 7.3cm x 2.5cm)

Heart Bear: 2⅜ inches W x 2 inches H x 1 inch D, excluding hanger (6cm x 5.1cm x 2.5cm)

Materials
- ¼ sheet 7-count plastic canvas
- Coats & Clark Red Heart Classic worsted weight yarn Art. E267 as listed in color key
- #16 tapestry needle
- 1½-inch (3.8cm) brown bear ornament
- 1½-inch (3.8cm) white bear ornament
- Hot-glue gun

Instructions
1. Cut plastic canvas according to graphs (page 94).
2. Stitch pieces following graphs, working uncoded areas on heart pieces with paddy green Continental Stitches.

3. When background stitching is completed, work jockey red French Knots on Santa's bag with full strand yarn. Work Backstitches and Straight Stitches on chimney pieces with 2 plies of white yarn.
4. Using paddy green, Overcast around top edges of hearts from dot to dot, then Whipstitch wrong sides of hearts together along remaining edges.

5. Using white, Whipstitch chimney front and back to chimney sides. Overcast top and bottom edges.
6. Using photo as a guide throughout, place hook of bag over chimney side; glue to back of chimney. Glue brown bear inside chimney and white bear inside heart pocket. ❧

GRAPH ON PAGE 94

Kaleidoscope Star

Beautiful multicolored beads shimmer and shine on this piece that will look just as pretty on your tree as in a window.

DESIGN BY GINA WOODS

Skill Level
Beginner

Size
5½ inches W x 5¾ inches H (14cm x 14.6cm)

Materials
- 1 (5-inch) Uniek QuickShape plastic canvas star
- Worsted weight yarn as listed in color key
- #16 tapestry needle
- 5 (2¼ x 2¾-inch/5.7 x 7cm) pieces from transparent plastic sheets in 5 different colors
- 25mm crystal starflake bead
- 5 (12mm) crystal starflake beads
- 6 (6mm) transparent faceted beads in colors similar to plastic sheets
- 5 (1⅜-inch/3.5cm) lengths 3mm fused crystal beads
- Hand-sewing needle
- White sewing thread
- Hot-glue gun

Instructions
1. Cut plastic canvas according to graph (page 95), cutting away gray areas. Do not cut off hanger section.

2. From each piece colored transparent plastic sheet, cut one diamond shape one bar larger all around than openings cut in plastic canvas star.

3. Stitch and Overcast piece following graph, Overcasting hanging section also.

4. Glue 25mm starflake bead to center of star. Using hand-sewing needle and white thread, attach one 6mm bead between each point of 25mm bead.

5. Sew fused beads to star where indicated on graph, trimming as needed to fit.

6. Lightly glue diamond-shaped transparent plastic sheets behind openings on star, using glue sparingly to avoid warping plastic sheet.

7. Lightly glue one 12mm starflake bead to center of transparent plastic sheet in each diamond-shaped opening. 🌿

GRAPHS ON PAGE 95

Chubby Cherubs

Select the embellishments of your choice to dress up this whimsical little trio of cherubs!

DESIGNS BY DEBRA ARCH

Skill Level
Intermediate

Size
4 inches W x 3⅛ inches H x 1⅜ inches D (10.2cm x 8cm x 3.5cm)

Materials
Each
- ⅓ sheet 7-count plastic canvas
- 2 (6-inch) Uniek QuickShape plastic canvas hearts
- 1 (4-inch) Uniek QuickShape plastic canvas radial circle
- Uniek Needloft plastic canvas yarn as listed in color key
- Kreinik ⅛-inch Ribbon as listed in color key
- #16 tapestry needle
- 2 (5mm) round black cabochons
- 1-inch/2.5cm-wide bow to coordinate with body color
- Blush
- Cotton swab
- Invisible thread
- Hot-glue gun

Purple Cherub
- 5 inches (12.7cm) ¼-inch/
- 0.6cm-wide white star garland
- 1 x ⅝-inch (2.5 x 1.6cm) piece white card stock
- Black fine-point felt-tip pen
- Decorative-edge scissors (optional)

Blue Cherub
- 5 inches (12.7cm) ¼-inch/ 0.6cm-wide silver tinsel garland
- ¾-inch (1.9cm) silver star

White Cherub
- 5 inches (12.7cm) ¼-inch/ 0.6cm-wide gold star garland
- ¾-inch (1.9cm) gold star

Cutting, Stitching & Assembly

1. Cut plastic canvas according to graphs (page 84), cutting away gray areas on body/head and arm pieces (hearts).

2. Following graphs throughout all stitching, stitch and Overcast arms, reversing one arm for each cherub before stitching. Stitch one set of arms with amethyst as graphed for purple cherub, one set replacing amethyst with sapphire for blue cherub and one set replacing amethyst with white for white cherub.

3. Stitch two body/head pieces and one base as graphed for purple cherub. Stitch two body/head pieces and one base replacing amethyst with sapphire for blue cherub, and two body/head pieces and one base replacing amethyst with white for white cherub.

4. Stitch two wings with white as graphed for purple cherub, two with silver for blue cherub and two with gold for white cherub.

5. Whipstitch wrong sides of corresponding wings together. Overcast both sides of each body/head piece from blue dot to blue dot with adjacent colors.

6. Whipstitch wrong sides of corresponding heads together around top from blue dot to blue dot. Insert wings in body/head, then

Whipstitch remaining side edges of bodies together. Whipstitch bases to bodies.

Finishing

1. Using photo as a guide throughout finishing, glue arms to body fronts along side edges at brackets.

2. Glue stars in place between hands on blue and white cherubs. Using felt-tip pen, write name on card stock. If desired, trim edges of card stock with decorative-edge scissors. Glue to front between hands on purple cherub.

3. Glue cabochons to heads for eyes where indicated. Glue tinsel and star garlands to heads for

halos. Glue bows to center front at necklines.

4. Using cotton swab, lightly apply blush to cheek areas.

5. For each hanger, thread a 9-inch (22.9cm) length of invisible thread behind top three center stitches on back of head. Tie ends together in a knot to form a loop for hanging. 🌿

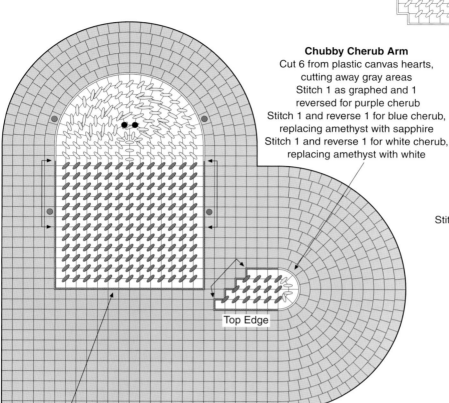

Chubby Cherub Arm
Cut 6 from plastic canvas hearts,
cutting away gray areas
Stitch 1 as graphed and 1
reversed for purple cherub
Stitch 1 and reverse 1 for blue cherub,
replacing amethyst with sapphire
Stitch 1 and reverse 1 for white cherub,
replacing amethyst with white

Chubby Cherubs Wings
23 holes x 23 holes
Cut 6
Stitch 2 as graphed for purple cherub
Stitch 2 replacing pearl
with silver for blue cherub
Stitch 2 replacing pearl
with gold for white cherub

Top Edge

Chubby Cherub Body/Head
Cut 6 from plastic canvas hearts,
cutting away gray areas
Stitch 2 as graphed for purple cherub
Stitch 2 for blue cherub,
replacing amethyst with sapphire
Stitch 2 for white cherub,
replacing amethyst with white

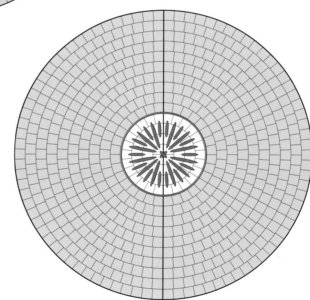

Chubby Cherubs Base
Cut 3 from 4-inch radial circles,
cutting away gray area
Stitch 1 as graphed for purple cherub
Stitch 1 replacing amethyst with
sapphire for blue cherub
Stitch 1 replacing amethyst with
white for white cherub

COLOR KEY

Yards	Plastic Canvas Yarn
18 (16.5m)	☐ Pale peach #56
	⅛-Inch Ribbon
14 (12.9m)	Silver hi lustre #001HL
14 (12.9m)	Gold hi lustre #002HL
21 (19.3m)	■ Amethyst #026
14 (12.9m)	☐ Pearl #032
21 (19.3m)	Sapphire hi lustre #051HL
21 (19.3m)	White #100
	● Attach black cabochon

Color numbers given are for Uniek Needloft
plastic canvas yarn and Kreinik ⅛-inch
Ribbon.

Holiday Lights

The look of glowing holiday lights is mimicked by the bright beads and pearls decorating this pretty tree.

DESIGN BY GINA WOODS

Skill Level
Beginner

Size
4⅜ inches W x 6 inches H
(11.1cm x 15.2cm)

Materials
- ¼ sheet 7-count plastic canvas
- Worsted weight yarn as listed in color key
- #16 tapestry needle
- 14 (6mm) beads in various colors
- 13mm gold sparkle star pony bead
- ½ yard (0.5m) 4mm clear iridescent fused beads
- 8 inches (20.3cm) ⅛-inch/ 3mm-wide gold satin ribbon
- Hand-sewing needle
- White sewing thread

Instructions
1. Cut plastic canvas according to graph (page 95).
2. Stitch and Overcast tree following graph.
3. Using hand-sewing needle and white thread, attach 6mm beads and star pony bead where indicated. Sew fused beads around edges of tree, where indicated.

4. For hanger, thread one end of gold ribbon from back to front through hole indicated, then up through star pony bead. Tie ends together in a bow to form a loop for hanging. Trim ends as desired. ❧

GRAPH ON PAGE 95

Cookie Cutouts

Calorie-free, you can enjoy these yummy-looking cookies guilt free!

DESIGNS BY GINA WOODS

Skill Level
Beginner

Size
Christmas Tree: 2¾ inches W x 3½ inches H (7cm x 8.9cm)

Gingerbread Boy: 2½ inches W x 3⅝ inches H (6.4cm x 9.2cm)

Star: 3½ inches W x 3⅜ inches H (8.9cm x 8.6cm)

Materials
- ¼ sheet 7-count plastic canvas
- 1 (5-inch) Uniek QuickShape plastic canvas star
- Worsted weight yarn as listed in color key
- 6-strand embroidery floss as listed in color key
- #16 tapestry needle
- 25 tiny bugle beads: red, green and silver
- 5 (4.5mm) black rocaille beads
- 7 each (5mm) pony beads: red and green
- 3 (8-inch/20.3cm) lengths ⅛-inch/3mm-wide gold satin ribbon
- Hand-sewing needle
- Black, white and spring green sewing thread

Instructions
1. Cut plastic canvas according to graphs (page 96), cutting away gray area on star.

2. Stitch and Overcast pieces following graphs, working uncoded areas on tree with spring green Continental Stitches and uncoded areas on gingerbread boy with dark gold Continental Stitches.

3. When background stitching is completed, work red floss Backstitches for mouth on gingerbread boy.

4. Using hand-sewing needle and spring green thread, attach green and red pony beads as desired to green area of tree. Use black thread to attach black beads to gingerbread boy where indicated and white thread to attach bugle beads as desired to white area of star.

5. For hanger on tree and gingerbread boy, thread one 8-inch (20.3cm) length each of gold ribbon from front to back through holes indicated at top. Tie ends together in a bow to form a loop for hanging. Repeat for star, threading remaining gold ribbon through hole indicated. Trim ends as desired. 🦅

GRAPHS ON PAGE 96

Sunbonnet Friends

Bright metallic ribbon and braid adds an updated look to the classic beauty of these country motifs.

DESIGNS BY MARY T. COSGROVE

Skill Level
Beginner

Size
Boy: 2⅝ inches W x 3⅜ inches H (6.7cm x 8.6cm)

Girl: 3⅜ inches W x 2⅝ inches H (8.6cm x 6.7cm)

Materials
- ¼ sheet white 7-count plastic canvas
- Kreinik ⅛-inch Ribbon as listed in color key
- Kreinik Fine (#8) Braid as listed in color key
- #16 tapestry needle

Instructions
1. Cut plastic canvas according to graphs (page 97).
2. Stitch pieces following graphs, working uncoded backgrounds with star yellow Continental Stitches; Overcast edges with star yellow while stitching. Do not work star yellow Continental Stitches under Straight Stitches on tree except where indicated and do not Overcast white squares around edges.
3. When background stitching is completed, work green ribbon Straight Stitches for tree and red ribbon Backstitches and Straight Stitches for lettering and at top of wreath. Work black fine (#8) braid Backstitches and Straight Stitches last.
4. Keeping ribbon smooth and flat, weave ribbon through white squares around edges. For woven green ribbon on girl and woven red ribbon on boy, leave a 3-inch (7.6cm) tail at beginning (green dot) and at end (red dot). Tie these tails together in a bow at top. 🌿

GRAPHS ON PAGE 97

Ear Ornaments

Dress up your ears with your choice of mittens, stockings or bells. These fun earrings are accented with pretty metallic beads.

DESIGNS BY MARY T. COSGROVE

Skill Level
Beginner

Size
Bells: 1⅛ inches W x 2⅛ inches H (2.9cm x 5.4cm)

Mittens: 1¼ inches W x 2¼ inches H (3.2cm x 5.7cm)

Stockings: 1 inch W x 2¼ inches H (2.5cm x 5.7cm)

Materials
- ¼ sheet 7-count plastic canvas
- Uniek Needloft plastic canvas yarn as listed in color key
- #16 tapestry needle
- 6 inches (15.2cm) each 24-gauge craft wire: purple, red and white
- 6 gold fish hook ear wires
- 4mm metallic beads:
    22 red
    20 purple
    2 gold
- Needle-nose pliers
- Wire cutters

Cutting & Stitching
1. Cut plastic canvas according to graphs. Cut each length of craft wire in half.

2. Stitch pieces following graphs, reversing two stockings and two mittens before stitching.

3. When background stitching is completed, work red Straight Stitches on bells and purple Backstitches on stockings.

Bell Earrings
1. Whipstitch wrong sides of two bell pieces together with purple yarn.

2. Using needle-nose pliers as needed, wrap one end of one length purple craft wire, around plastic canvas where indicated with arrow; twist to hold in place.

3. Thread on beads as follows: three red, one purple, three red. Bring end of wire though loop on one ear wire: twist to hold. Cut excess.

4. Use excess wire to add 4mm gold bead to bottom of bell where indicated on graph.

5. Repeat steps 1–4 for second earring.

Mitten Earrings
1. Using red yarn, Whipstitch

wrong sides of two mitten pieces together, matching edges.

2. Using needle-nose pliers as needed, wrap one end of one length white craft wire around plastic canvas where indicated with arrow; twist to hold in place.

3. Thread on beads as follows: three purple, one red, three purple. Bring end of wire though loop on one ear wire: twist to hold. Cut excess.

4. Repeat steps 1–3 for second earring.

Stocking Earrings
1. Using white yarn, Whipstitch wrong sides of two stocking pieces together, matching edges.

2. Using needle-nose pliers as needed, wrap one end of one length red craft wire, around plastic canvas where indicated with arrow; twist to hold in place.

3. Thread on beads as follows: one red, one purple, one red, one purple, one red, one purple, one red. Bring end of wire though loop on one ear wire: twist to hold. Cut excess.

4. Repeat steps 1–3 for second earring. ❧

Ho, Ho, Ho

Create jolly Santas to decorate your home and embellish your gifts. He is the personification of the spirit of holiday giving.

Santa Triptych

This trio of handsome old-world Santas are Whipstitched together to create the hinged look of a triptych.

DESIGN BY KATHY WIRTH

Skill Level
Intermediate

Size
11¾ inches W x 9⅛ inches H
(29.8cm x 23.2cm)

Materials
- 1¼ sheets stiff 7-count plastic canvas
- 1 sheet white 7-count plastic canvas
- Coats & Clark Red Heart Classic worsted weight yarn Art. E267 as listed in color key
- Coats & Clark Red Heart Kids worsted weight yarn Art. E711 as listed in color key
- 6-strand embroidery floss as listed in color key
- #16 tapestry needle
- #18 tapestry needle
- 3 (¼-inch/1cm) black buttons
- 3 (1½-inch/3.8cm) wood stars
- 2¼ x ⅛-inch (5.7 x 0.3cm) match stick
- 3 (½-inch/13mm) white iridescent pompoms
- Medium yellow acrylic craft paint
- Paintbrush
- Hot-glue gun

Project Note
Use #16 tapestry needle for yarn and #18 tapestry needle for 6-strand embroidery floss.

Instructions
1. Cut Santas, arms, mustaches and signs from stiff plastic canvas according to graphs (pages 101, 102 and 103), cutting Santas without hinges, using blue lines at hinges as edges.

2. Cut Santas with hinges from white plastic canvas for backing. Backing will remain unstitched.

3. Paint stars and match stick with medium yellow paint. Allow to dry.

4. Stitch stiff plastic canvas pieces following graphs, leaving blue lines and areas indicated on Santas unworked. Work uncoded backgrounds on signs with white Continental Stitches.

5. When background stitching is completed, work lettering on signs with black floss. Work white French Knots on right Santa's hat and black floss French Knots for eyes on all Santas. Using black floss, attach black buttons to left Santa where indicated on graph.

6. Overcast bottom edges of Santa front pieces. Overcast all arms, mustaches and signs.

7. Place backing pieces behind Santas and Whipstitch together, working Continental Stitches along blue lines through both layers of canvas, but leaving hinges and bottom side edges from dot to dot of middle Santa unworked.

8. Whipstitch top hinges together with jockey red. Using white, Whipstitch bottom hinges of left and right Santas to bottom side edges of middle Santa.

9. Using photo as a guide throughout, glue match stick behind one star. Glue pompoms, mustaches, arms, stars and signs to Santas. ❧

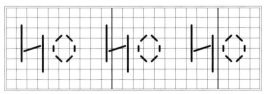

Left & Right Santa Sign
24 holes x 8 holes
Cut 2 from stiff

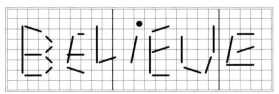

Middle Santa Sign
25 holes x 8 holes
Cut 1 from stiff

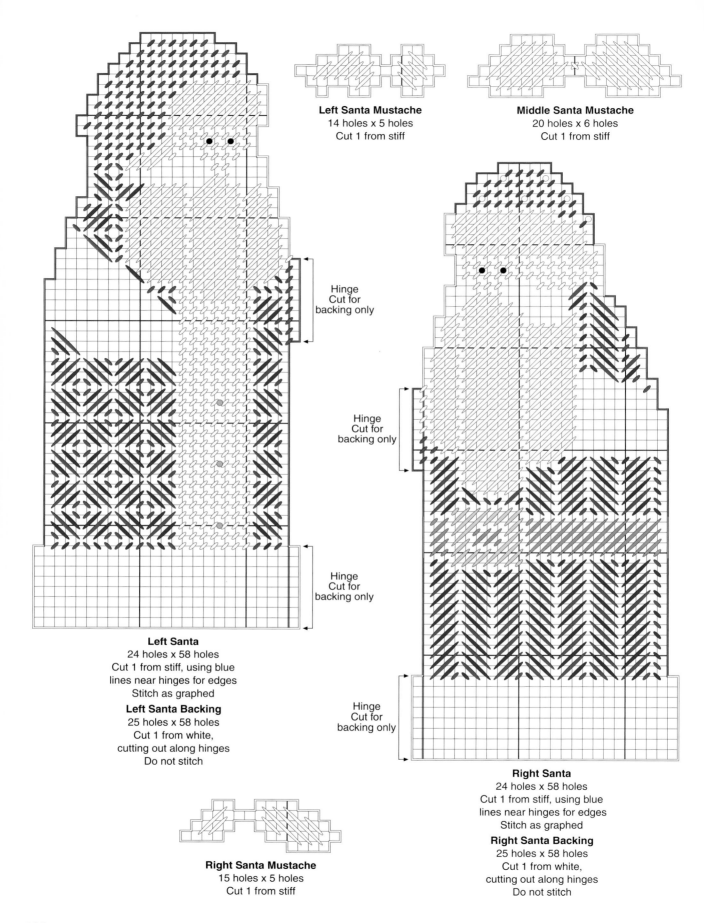

Left Santa Mustache
14 holes x 5 holes
Cut 1 from stiff

Middle Santa Mustache
20 holes x 6 holes
Cut 1 from stiff

Hinge
Cut for
backing only

Hinge
Cut for
backing only

Hinge
Cut for
backing only

Hinge
Cut for
backing only

Left Santa
24 holes x 58 holes
Cut 1 from stiff, using blue
lines near hinges for edges
Stitch as graphed

Left Santa Backing
25 holes x 58 holes
Cut 1 from white,
cutting out along hinges
Do not stitch

Right Santa Mustache
15 holes x 5 holes
Cut 1 from stiff

Right Santa
24 holes x 58 holes
Cut 1 from stiff, using blue
lines near hinges for edges
Stitch as graphed

Right Santa Backing
25 holes x 58 holes
Cut 1 from white,
cutting out along hinges
Do not stitch

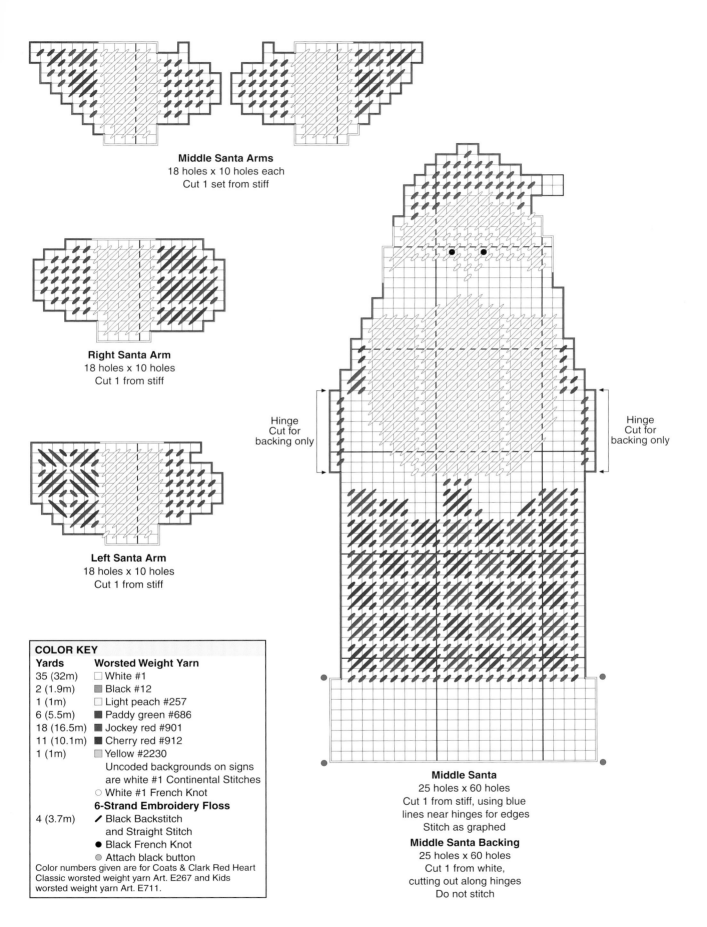

Middle Santa Arms
18 holes x 10 holes each
Cut 1 set from stiff

Right Santa Arm
18 holes x 10 holes
Cut 1 from stiff

Left Santa Arm
18 holes x 10 holes
Cut 1 from stiff

Hinge
Cut for
backing only

Hinge
Cut for
backing only

COLOR KEY

Yards	Worsted Weight Yarn
35 (32m)	☐ White #1
2 (1.9m)	▨ Black #12
1 (1m)	☐ Light peach #257
6 (5.5m)	■ Paddy green #686
18 (16.5m)	■ Jockey red #901
11 (10.1m)	■ Cherry red #912
1 (1m)	▨ Yellow #2230

Uncoded backgrounds on signs
are white #1 Continental Stitches
○ White #1 French Knot
6-Strand Embroidery Floss

4 (3.7m)	✒ Black Backstitch and Straight Stitch
	● Black French Knot
	◉ Attach black button

Color numbers given are for Coats & Clark Red Heart
Classic worsted weight yarn Art. E267 and Kids
worsted weight yarn Art. E711.

Middle Santa
25 holes x 60 holes
Cut 1 from stiff, using blue
lines near hinges for edges
Stitch as graphed
Middle Santa Backing
25 holes x 60 holes
Cut 1 from white,
cutting out along hinges
Do not stitch

Santa Shelf Sitter

Piping cord wrapped with red yarn creates the flexible arms and legs on this lanky shelf sitter that'll look right at home on your mantle or counter!

DESIGN BY LEE LINDEMAN

Skill Level

Intermediate

Size

Sitting: Approximately 6¼ inches W x 15 inches H x 5½ inches D (15.9cm x 38.1cm x 14cm)

Materials

- 1 sheet 7-count plastic canvas
- Uniek Needloft plastic canvas yarn as listed in color key
- #16 tapestry needle
- Small amounts white and red craft foam
- 26 inches (66cm) ⅜-inch (9mm) piping cord
- 2 (4mm) black beads
- 5 (½-inch/13mm) white pompoms
- ⅝ x ⅜-inch (1.6 x 1cm) gold belt buckle
- Small amount black felt or faux suede
- White faux fur
- Polyester fiberfill
- Small stones for weights in mittens and boots
- Large stones for weight in body
- Child's red sock
- Hand-sewing needle
- Red sewing thread
- Hot-glue gun

Cutting & Stitching

1. Cut plastic canvas according to graphs (pages 106 and 107), cutting out holes in boot tops.

2. Cut one mustache from white craft foam, using pattern given. Cut one ³⁄₁₆-inch (0.5cm) circle from red craft foam for nose.

3. From white faux fur, cut one beard using pattern given. Cut one 3½ x 1-inch (8.9 x 2.5cm) strip for back hair and one 4 x ½-inch (10.2 x 1.3cm) strip for front hair from white faux fur.

4. Cut one ¾ x ⅜-inch (1.9 x 1cm) strip black felt or faux suede for belt buckle.

5. For hat, cut 3 inches (7.6cm) off cuff from child's red sock; turn inside out. Using hand-sewing needle and red thread, sew a running stitch along cut edge of cuff; pull thread to gather, then knot thread. Turn right side out. Set aside.

6. Stitch pieces following graphs, reversing two mittens before stitching.

7. Overcast inside edges of boot tops. Overcast top edges of mittens from blue dot to blue dot and top edges of body pieces from blue dot to blue dot.

8. Overcast body edges (for arms and legs) inside brackets. Overcast body base edges inside brackets.

Arms & Legs

1. From piping cord, cut two 5-inch (12.7cm) lengths for arms and two 8-inch (20.3cm) lengths for legs.

2. Wrap entire lengths of both arms and legs tightly with red yarn, gluing ends to secure. Set aside.

Assembly

1. Whipstitch wrong sides of head front and back together, filling with fiberfill before closing.

2. Matching edges, Whipstitch two mittens together around side and bottom edges. Repeat with remaining two mitten pieces.

3. Place a few small stones inside one mitten, then glue end of one arm inside mitten. Repeat with remaining arm and mitten.

4. Whipstitch side edges of body front and back together at shoulders, then glue arms in body, making sure thumbs of mittens are facing in. Whipstitch remaining side edges of body pieces together.

5. Glue neck of head inside

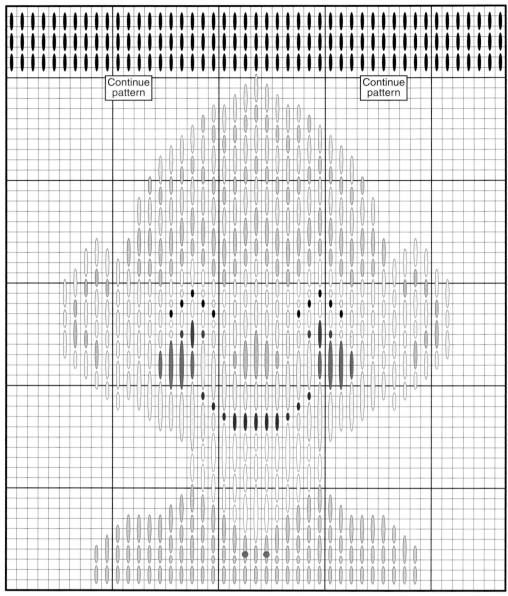

Elf Portrait
47 holes x 57 holes
Cut 1

COLOR KEY	
ELF PORTRAIT	
Yards	**Plastic Canvas Yarn**
6 (5.5m)	■ Red #01
1 (1m)	▨ Lavender #05
1 (1m)	▨ Camel #43
6 (5.5m)	☐ Pale peach #56
	Worsted Weight Yarn
7 (6.5m)	☐ White multi #301 (2 strands)
20 (18.3m)	■ Black #312
1 (1m)	■ Burgundy #376
15 (13.8m)	▨ Medium thyme #406
10 (9.2m)	☐ Frosty green #661
10 (9.2m)	■ Dark thyme #2675
	● Attach red ribbon

Color numbers given are for Uniek Needloft
plastic canvas yarn, Lion Brand Yarn Wool-Ease
worsted weight yarn Article 620, and Coats &
Clark Red Heart Super Saver worsted weight
yarn Art. E300 and TLC Essentials worsted
weight yarn Art. E514.

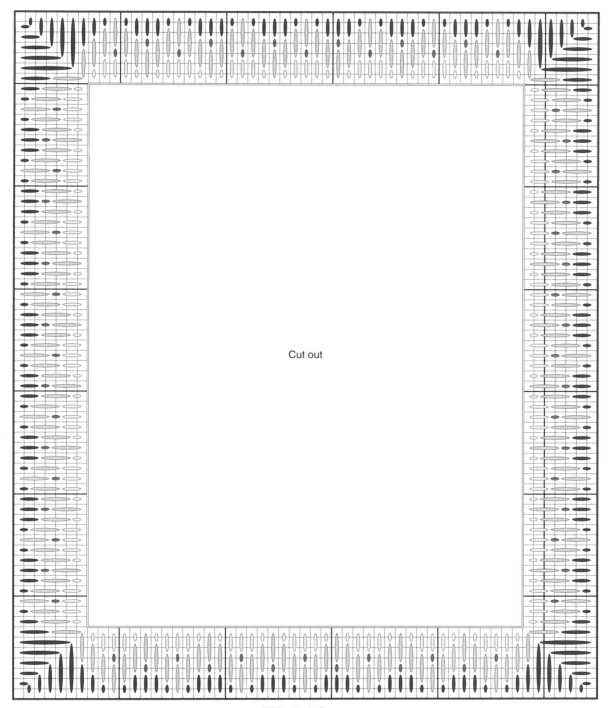

Cut out

Elf Portrait Frame
55 holes x 67 holes
Cut 1

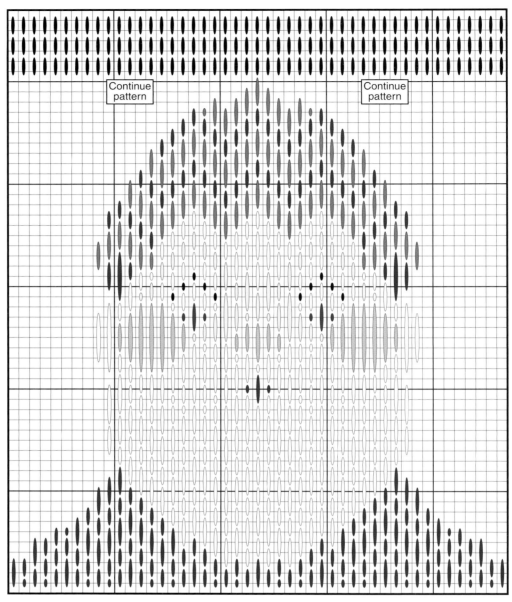

Continue pattern

Continue pattern

Santa Portrait
47 holes x 57 holes
Cut 1

COLOR KEY
SANTA PORTRAIT

Yards	Plastic Canvas Yarn
2 (1.9m)	▨ Lavender #05
2 (1.9m)	☐ Pale peach #56
	Worsted Weight Yarn
20 (18.3m)	☐ White multi #301 (2 strands)
20 (18.3m)	■ Black #312
12 (11m)	▨ Cherry red #319
15 (13.8m)	■ Burgundy #376
1 (1m)	▨ Medium thyme #406
10 (9.2m)	☐ Frosty green #661
3 (2.8m)	■ Dark thyme #2675

Color numbers given are for Uniek Needloft plastic canvas yarn, Lion Brand Yarn Wool-Ease worsted weight yarn Article 620, and Coats & Clark Red Heart Super Saver worsted weight yarn Art. E300 and TLC Essentials worsted weight yarn Art. E514.

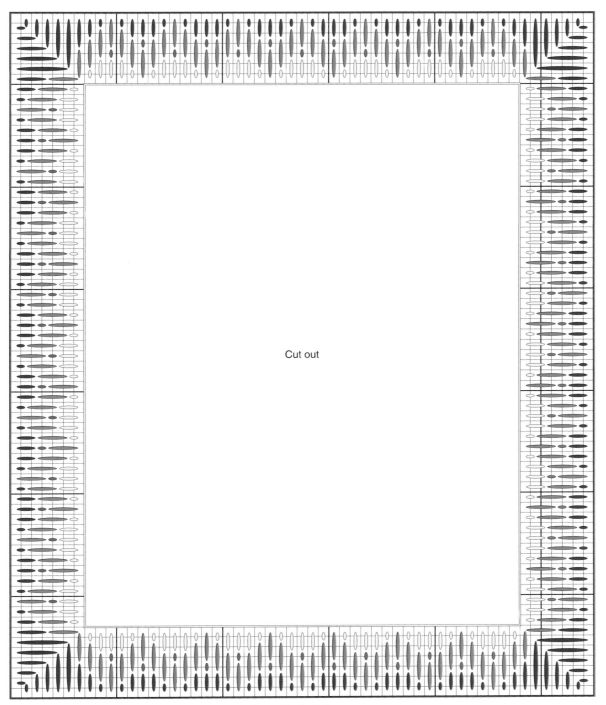

Santa Portrait Frame
55 holes x 67 holes
Cut 1

Treat Mat

Serve Santa his milk and cookies in style this year with a personalized mat decorated with dimensional holly leaves.

DESIGN BY BETTY HANSEN

Skill Level
Beginner

Size
13½ inches W x 10½ inches H
(34.4cm x 26.7cm)

Materials
- 1¼ sheets clear 7-count plastic canvas
- 1 sheet white 7-count plastic canvas
- Worsted weight yarn as listed in color key
- Uniek Needloft iridescent craft cord as listed in color key
- #16 tapestry needle

Instructions

1. Cut holly leaves from ¼ sheet plastic canvas according to graphs. Do not cut remaining clear and white plastic canvas sheets. White sheet will remain unstitched.

2. Stitch and Overcast holly leaves following graphs, working green Straight Stitches when stitching and Overcasting are completed.

3. Using one entire sheet clear plastic canvas, stitch mat following both left and right side graphs (pages 116 and 117), working borders first and working uncoded areas on white background with white Continental Stitches and uncoded areas on peach background with light peach Continental Stitches. Work cuff on hat with double strand white yarn.

4. When background stitching is completed, work black iridescent craft cord Straight Stitches for eyes. Use double strand pink to Straight Stitch nose. Embroider eyebrows, mustache and top part of beard with white.

5. Work white French Knots for pompom on Santa's hat and red French Knots for holly berries on each side of Santa.

6. Place holly leaves on mat where indicated with blue lines, then attach to mat with red French Knots where indicated on holly leaves graph.

7. Place white plastic canvas sheet behind stitched mat and Whipstitch together with red. 🎄

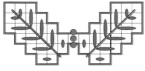

Treat Mat Holly Leaves
13 holes x 6 holes
Cut 4

COLOR KEY	
Yards	**Worsted Weight Yarn**
41 (37.5m)	☐ White
15 (13.8m)	■ Red
15 (13.8m)	■ Green
1 (1m)	☐ Pink
	Uncoded areas on white background are white Continental Stitches
2 (1.9m)	Uncoded areas on peach background are light peach Continental Stitches
	∕ White Backstitch and Straight Stitch
	∕ Pink Straight Stitch
	∕ Green Straight Stitch
	○ White French Knot
	● Red French Knot
	Iridescent Craft Cord
1 (1m)	∕ Black #55048 Straight Stitch
Color number given is for Uniek Needloft iridescent craft cord.	

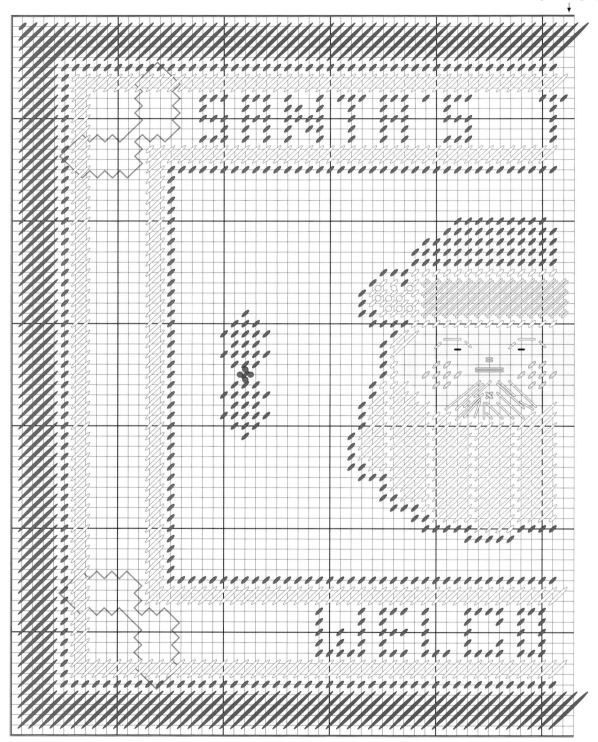

Treat Mat Left Side
90 holes x 70 holes
Stitch 1 clear sheet, following
both left and right side graphs

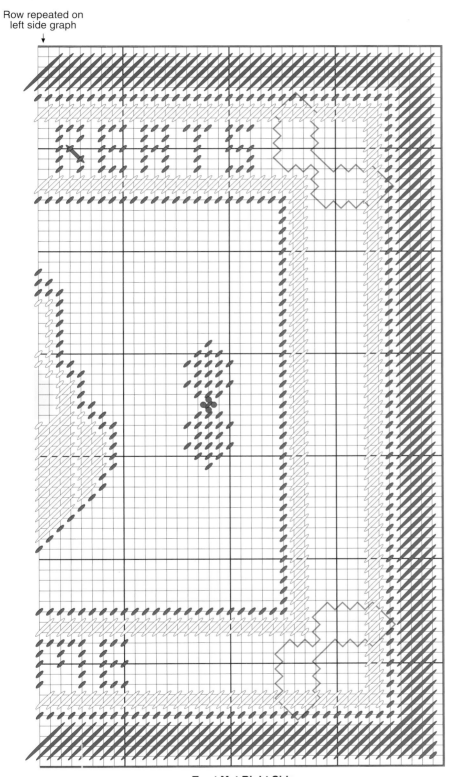

Treat Mat Right Side
90 holes x 70 holes
Stitch 1 clear sheet, following
both left and right side graphs

Jolly St. Nick

Store your favorite holiday candies and treats in this delightful Santa catchall that's complete with removable top.

DESIGN BY BETTY HANSEN

Skill Level

Intermediate

Size

Approximately 7⅝ inches W x 6⅝ inches H x 4 inches D, including top (19.4cm x 16.8cm x 10.2cm)

Materials

- 1 sheet 7-count plastic canvas
- 4 (5-inch) Uniek QuickShape plastic canvas hearts
- Worsted weight yarn as listed in color key
- Uniek Needloft iridescent craft cord as listed in color key
- #16 tapestry needle
- 4 (½-inch/13mm) gold jingle bells
- 2 (¾-inch/19mm) gold jingle bells
- 1-inch (25mm) gold jingle bell

Cutting & Stitching

1. Cut plastic canvas according to graphs (pages 119, 120 and 121). Do not cut plastic canvas hearts.

2. Following graphs throughout all stitching, stitch and Overcast holly leaves and mustache. Stitch base, hat and hat support pieces. Stitch one plastic canvas heart each for front and back, working uncoded areas on front with light tan Continental Stitches. Remaining hearts will be used for liners and will not be stitched.

3. When background stitching is completed, work green Straight Stitches on holly leaves and white French Knots on front for Santa's eyebrows, wrapping needle two times.

Assembly

1. Matching colors, Whipstitch two base pieces together along short edges, forming one long strip. Overcast remaining short edges.

2. Place mustache on front (see photo), then tack in place with white yarn where indicated on mustache graph.

3. Place unstitched hearts behind stitched front and back, then Whipstitch white side of base to front and front liner from dot to dot easing as necessary to fit. Whipstitch remaining top edges of front and front liner together.

4. Whipstitch red side of base to back and back liner from dot to dot, easing as necessary to fit. Whipstitch remaining top edges of back and back liner together.

5. Whipstitch two hat pieces together along top edges. Whipstitch top edges of hat support pieces to side edges of hat pieces at peak. Overcast all remaining edges of assembled hat.

6. Using red yarn through step 7, attach 1-inch (25mm) jingle bell to peak of hat where indicated. Place holly leaves on hat pieces around jingle bell as indicated with blue lines. Attach each with three French Knots, wrapping needle two times.

7. Attach remaining jingle bells to bottom edge of hat pieces where indicated on graph. 🌿

COLOR KEY

Yards	Worsted Weight Yarn
48 (43.9m)	■ Red
20 (19.3m)	☐ White
2 (1.9m)	■ Green
1 (1m)	☐ Pink
4 (3.7m)	Uncoded areas on head front are light tan Continental Stitches
	╱ Green Straight Stitch
	● Red (2-wrap) French Knot
	○ White (2-wrap) French Knot
	Iridescent Craft Cord
1 (1m)	■ Black #55048
	╱ Attach mustache
	● Attach 1/2-inch (13mm) jingle bell
	○ Attach 3/4-inch (19mm) jingle bell
	○ Attach 1-inch (25mm) jingle bell

Color number given is for Uniek Needloft iridescent craft cord.

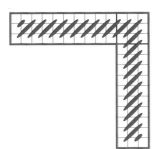

Jolly St. Nick Hat Support
13 holes x 13 holes
Cut 2

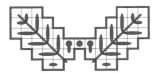

Jolly St. Nick Holly Leaves
13 holes x 6 holes
Cut 2

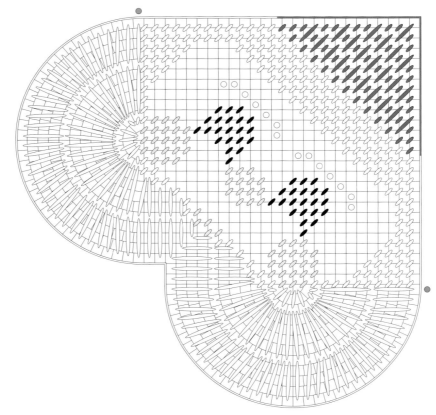

Jolly St. Nick Front
Stitch 1

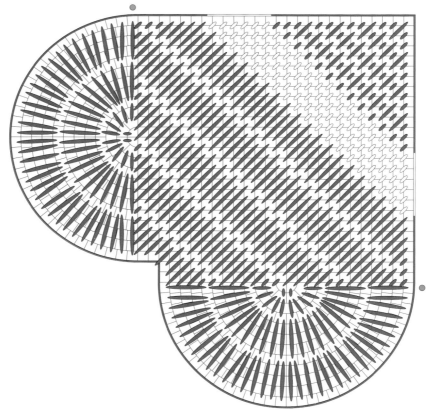

Jolly St. Nick Back
Stitch 1

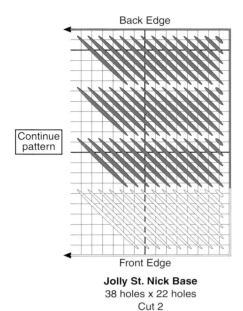

Back Edge

Continue pattern

Front Edge

Jolly St. Nick Base
38 holes x 22 holes
Cut 2

COLOR KEY

Yards	Worsted Weight Yarn
48 (43.9m)	■ Red
20 (19.3m)	☐ White
2 (1.9m)	■ Green
1 (1m)	☐ Pink
4 (3.7m)	Uncoded areas on head front are light tan Continental Stitches
	✎ Green Straight Stitch
	● Red (2-wrap) French Knot
	○ White (2-wrap) French Knot
Iridescent Craft Cord	
1 (1m)	■ Black #55048
	✎ Attach mustache
	● Attach ¹/₂-inch (13mm) jingle bell
	○ Attach ³/₄-inch (19mm) jingle bell
	○ Attach 1-inch (25mm) jingle bell

Color number given is for Uniek Needloft iridescent craft cord.

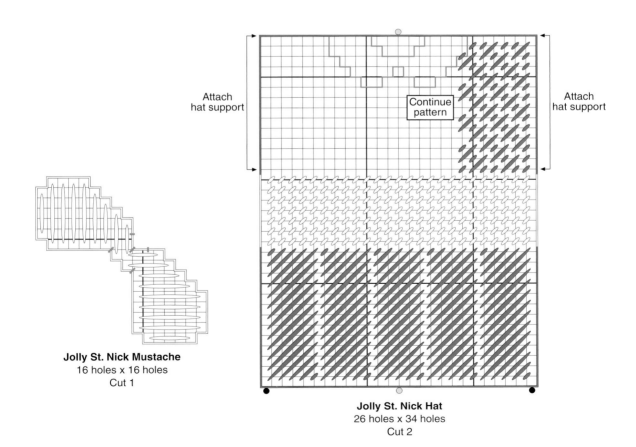

Attach hat support

Continue pattern

Attach hat support

Jolly St. Nick Mustache
16 holes x 16 holes
Cut 1

Jolly St. Nick Hat
26 holes x 34 holes
Cut 2

Gift Card Holder

Delight that special someone with a gift card to a favorite store presented in a handmade plastic canvas holder.

DESIGN BY CYNTHIA ROBERTS

Skill Level
Beginner

Size
3⅞ inches W x 3⅛ inches H (9.8cm x 8cm)

Materials
- ½ sheet 7-count plastic canvas
- Worsted weight yarn as listed in color key
- #16 tapestry needle
- 15 inches (38.1cm) ⅛-inch/ 3mm-wide red satin ribbon

Instructions

1. Cut front and back from plastic canvas according to graph (page 127).

2. Stitch holder front as graphed. When background stitching is completed, work red Running Stitches.

3. Stitch holder back entirely in the green Slanted Gobelin Stitch and red Running Stitch pattern, eliminating Santa's head.

4. Using red throughout, Overcast top edges. Whipstitch wrong sides of front and back together around side and bottom edges.

5. Insert red ribbon through front and back in hole indicated and tie in a bow. Trim ends as desired.

GRAPH ON PAGE 127

Kris Kringle Napkin Rings

Add a little merriment to your next holiday meal with fun and festive Santa napkin rings complete with beads.

DESIGN BY MARY T. COSGROVE

Skill Level
Beginner

Size
Santa: 2 inches W x 2⅜ inches H (5.1cm x 6cm)

With Ring: 1¾ inches in diameter

Materials
- ¼ sheet 7-count plastic canvas
- Uniek Needloft plastic canvas yarn as listed in color key
- #16 tapestry needle
- 4 (6-inch/15.2cm) lengths 24-gauge black craft wire
- 48 (8mm) green plastic faceted beads
- Needle-nose pliers

Instructions

1. Cut plastic canvas according to graph (page 127).

2. Stitch and Overcast Santas following graph, working uncoded areas with red Continental Stitches.

3. When background stitching and Overcasting are completed, use single strand of yarn to work Backstitches and French Knots.

4. To attach ring to each Santa, thread end of one length of wire through hole indicated on one hand; twist end around wire to hold in place.

5. Thread on 12 green beads, bring wire around back of Santa to other hand and thread through hole indicated, twist end to secure. Trim wire ends as needed.

GRAPH ON PAGE 127

Holly Jolly Bathroom Tissue Cover

Hide that spare roll of tissue paper this holiday season with a Mr. Claus holder complete with movable eyes and fuzzy eyebrows.

DESIGN BY SANDRA MILLER MAXFIELD

Skill Level
Intermediate

Size
4¾ inches H x 5¼ inches in diameter (12.1cm x 13.3cm)

Materials
- 1 sheet 7-count plastic canvas
- Worsted weight yarn as listed in color key
- #16 tapestry needle
- 2 (15mm) movable eyes
- 15mm white bump chenille stem
- Hot-glue gun

Instructions

1. Cut plastic canvas according to graphs (pages 126 and 127).

2. Following graphs throughout all stitching, stitch and Overcast nose, mustache, beard curls and holly.

3. Stitch remaining pieces, overlapping three holes on each side of cover front with three holes on each side of cover back before stitching, forming 5¼-inch (13.3cm) circle. Stitch front as graphed; stitch back, eliminating light peach area for face and working the vertical off-white Slanted Gobelin Stitch pattern across back instead.

4. Overcast bottom edge of cover and around bottom and side edges of tassel from blue dot to blue dot.

5. Whipstitch top to cover, attaching tassel where indicated on front while Whipstitching.

6. Using photo as a guide through step 9, glue eyes to front where indicated with black circles, glue top of nose to face where indicated with pink line, then glue center top of mustache to face under nose.

7. Arrange four beard curls behind bottom edge of mustache, overlapping as needed. Place four more beard curls behind the first four, then place remaining five behind bottom four. Glue in place, gluing mustache on top. **Note:** *Bottom beard curls should be even with bottom edge of front so it is important to arrange beard curls before gluing in place.*

8. For one eyebrow, cut bump chenille stem so that widest part of one bump is above eye and tapered end of bump is to the side of eye. Bend to shape, then glue in place. Repeat for remaining eyebrow.

9. Glue holly to cover on left side of face front. 🍃

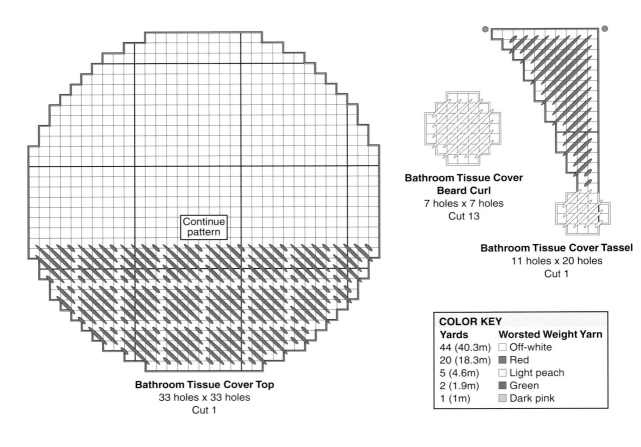

Bathroom Tissue Cover Top
33 holes x 33 holes
Cut 1

**Bathroom Tissue Cover
Beard Curl**
7 holes x 7 holes
Cut 13

Bathroom Tissue Cover Tassel
11 holes x 20 holes
Cut 1

COLOR KEY	
Yards	**Worsted Weight Yarn**
44 (40.3m)	☐ Off-white
20 (18.3m)	■ Red
5 (4.6m)	☐ Light peach
2 (1.9m)	■ Green
1 (1m)	☐ Dark pink

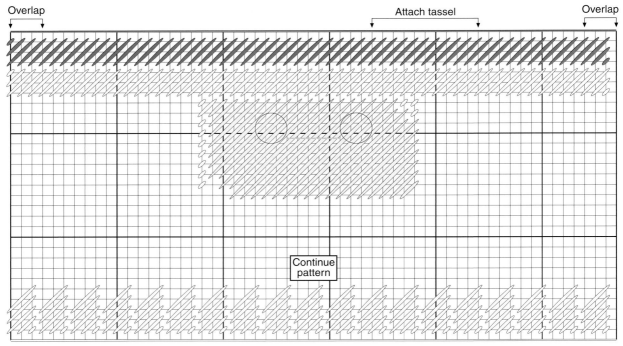

Bathroom Tissue Cover Front & Back
57 holes x 30 holes
Cut 2
Stitch front as graphed
Stitch back working the off-white
vertical stitch pattern across back
in place of light peach stitches

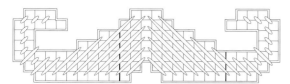

Bathroom Tissue Cover Mustache
25 holes x 7 holes
Cut 1

Bathroom Tissue Cover Nose
7 holes x 4 holes
Cut 1

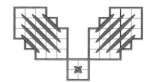

Bathroom Tissue Cover Holly
12 holes x 7 holes
Cut 1

Gift Card Holder

CONTINUED FROM PAGE 122

COLOR KEY	
Yards	**Worsted Weight Yarn**
9 (8.3m)	■ Green
5 (4.6m)	■ Red
1 (1m)	☐ White
1 (1m)	☐ Light peach
1 (1m)	■ Black
	╱ Red Running Stitch
	● Attach red ribbon

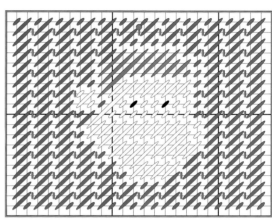

Gift Card Holder Front & Back
25 holes x 20 holes
Cut 2
Stitch front as graphed
Stitch back entirely in
green Slanted Gobelin Stitch
and red Running Stitch pattern

Kris Kringle Napkin Rings

CONTINUED FROM PAGE 123

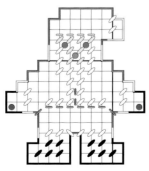

Napkin Ring Kris Kringle
13 holes x 15 holes
Cut 4

COLOR KEY	
Yards	**Plastic Canvas Yarn**
4 (3.7m)	■ Black #00
1 (1m)	☐ Pink #07
4 (3.7m)	☐ White #41
5 (4.6m)	Uncoded areas are red #01 Continental Stitches
	╱ Red #01 Overcast
	╱ Black #00 (1-ply) Backstitch
	╱ White #41 (1-ply) Backstitch
	● Black #00 (1-ply) French Knot
	● Red #01 (1-ply) French Knot
	● Attach wire for ring

Color numbers given are for Uniek Needloft
plastic canvas yarn.

Deck the Halls

Dress up your home this holiday season with one of these delightful decor pieces. From handy catch-alls to darling shelf sitters, you'll fall in love with each and every design.

Frosteen

Sweet as can be, this darling snow "woman" is just as cute whether used as a centerpiece or a sit-around.

DESIGN BY DEBRA ARCH

Skill Level
Intermediate

Size
7⅝ inches W x 9¼ inches H x 5 inches D (19.4cm x 23.5cm x 12.7cm)

Materials
- 2 sheets 7-count plastic canvas
- 2 (9-inch) Uniek QuickShape plastic canvas radial circles
- 1 (6-inch) Uniek QuickShape plastic canvas radial circle
- Lion Brand Wool-Ease worsted weight yarn Article 620 as listed in color key
- Kreinik ⅛-inch Ribbon as listed in color key
- Uniek Needloft solid metallic craft cord as listed in color key
- #16 tapestry needle
- Beading needle
- 9 black E beads
- 3 purple E beads
- 1-inch (2.5cm) white snowflake
- 2 yards (1.9m) ⅜-inch/1cm-wide iridescent mini star or snowflake garland
- Blush
- Cotton swab
- Black and white sewing thread
- Hot-glue gun

Instructions

1. Cut plastic canvas according to graphs (pages 132 and 133), cutting away yellow areas on 9-inch radial circles. Cut the three outermost rows of holes from 6-inch radial circle for base. Base will remain unstitched.

2. Following graphs throughout, stitch and Overcast nose. Stitch body, hat and hat brim pieces, using 2 strands white multi to stitch body and 2 strands periwinkle to stitch hat and hat brim pieces.

3. Using beading needle and black thread, attach black beads for eyes and mouth where indicated on graph, then use white thread to attach purple beads for buttons where indicated.

4. Whipstitch body pieces together around side and top edges, then Whipstitch body to unstitched base.

5. Overcast top edge of hat brim front from red dot to red dot, then with right sides facing front, Whipstitch hat brim front to one hat piece along bottom edges from blue dot to blue dot.

6. Overcast bottom edge of remaining hat, then Whipstitch wrong sides of hat pieces together around side and top edges, catching side edges of hat brim front while Whipstitching.

7. Use photo as a guide through step 9. For hatband, thread solid purple craft cord from back to front through holes indicated on hat, then tie cord in a bow and trim ends.

8. Glue nose to head where indicated on graph with blue lines. Use cotton swab to apply small amount of blush to cheeks.

9. Glue hat to head, then glue 1-inch (2.5cm) snowflake to hat. Wrap garland around body as desired and tack in place with glue. ❦

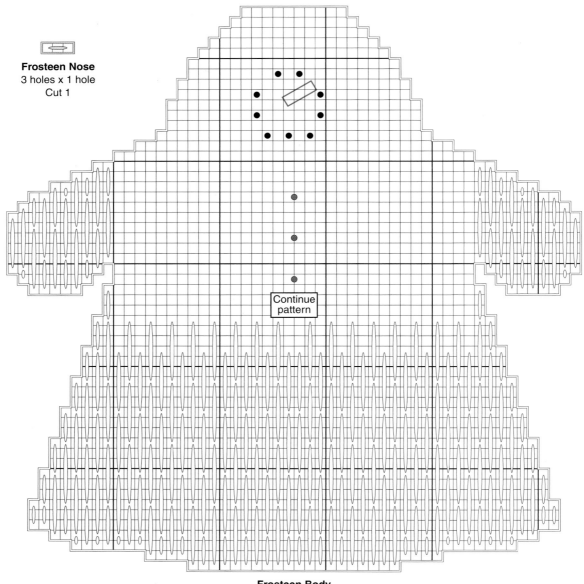

Frosteen Nose
3 holes x 1 hole
Cut 1

Continue
pattern

Frosteen Body
54 holes x 55 holes
Cut 2

COLOR KEY	
Yards	**Worsted Weight Yarn**
100 (91.5m)	☐ White multi #301 (2 strands)
	¹/₈-Inch Ribbon
1 (1m)	☐ Star pink #092
25 (22.9m)	☐ Periwinkle #9294 (2 strands)
	Solid Metallic Craft Cord
1 (1m)	○ Attach solid purple #55030 hatband
	● Attach black E bead
	● Attach purple E bead

Color numbers given are for Lion Brand Yarn
Wool-Ease worsted weight yarn Article 620,
Kreinik ¹/₈-inch Ribbon and Uniek Needloft solid
metallic craft cord.

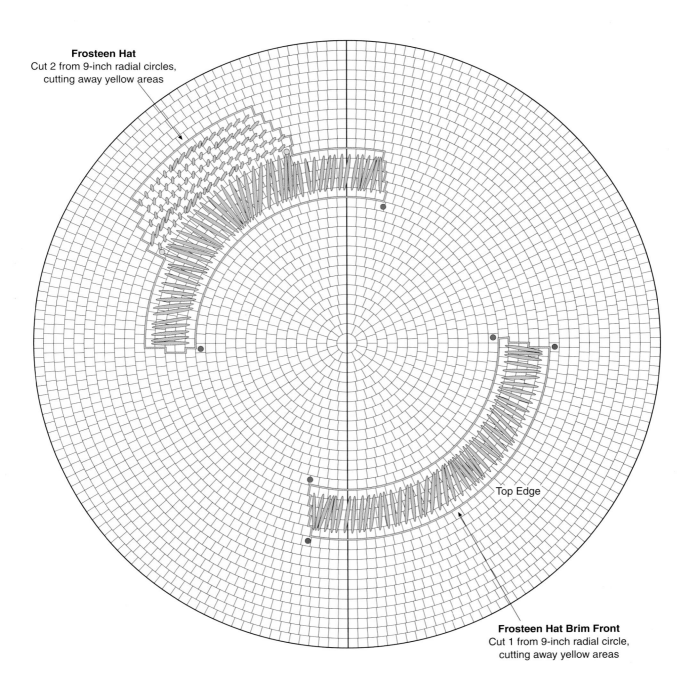

Frosteen Hat
Cut 2 from 9-inch radial circles,
cutting away yellow areas

Top Edge

Frosteen Hat Brim Front
Cut 1 from 9-inch radial circle,
cutting away yellow areas

Toy Soldier

Just as festive as a holiday nutcracker, this fellow will charm you this Christmas season.

DESIGN BY DEBRA ARCH

Skill Level
Beginner

Size
5¾ inches W x 10¾ inches H x 4 inches D (14.6cm x 27.3cm x 10.2cm)

Materials
- 1½ sheets 7-count plastic canvas
- 2 (4-inch) Uniek QuickShape plastic canvas radial circles
- 1 (9-inch) Uniek QuickShape plastic canvas radial circle
- 1 (6-inch) Uniek QuickShape plastic canvas heart
- Coats & Clark Red Heart Plush worsted weight yarn Art. E719 as listed in color key
- Coats & Clark Red Heart Super Saver worsted weight yarn Art. E300 as listed in color key
- Kreinik ⅛-inch Ribbon as listed in color key
- #16 tapestry needle
- Beading needle
- 2 (6mm) black cabochons
- 6 (8mm) round silver beads
- 6 (⅜-inch/1cm) silver stars
- 1-inch (2.5cm) silver star
- Blush
- Cotton swab
- 9⅛-inch/23.2cm-tall potato chip canister with lid
- 2 cups sand
- Hot-glue gun

Project Note
Use 2 strands bluebird yarn and 2 strands silver for all background stitching.

Instructions
1. Cut plastic canvas according to graphs (pages 136, 137 and 138), cutting away gray areas on 9-inch and 4-inch radial circles and on plastic canvas heart.

2. Following graphs throughout all stitching, stitch and Overcast chin strap, hat bill and bib. Stitch body, top and arms, working uncoded areas on body and arms with Aran Continental Stitches. Base will remain unstitched.

3. Whipstitch side edges of body together, forming back seam, then Whipstitch top to body.

4. Fill potato chip canister with sand, then glue on lid. Insert canister in body. Whipstitch unstitched base to body with black.

5. Fold arms in half where indicated and Whipstitch around side and bottom edges. Place one shoulder on top edge of each arm with narrow end at seam, then Whipstitch in place.

6. Using photo as a guide through step 9, glue seam side of arms to coat on body over horizontal stitches. Glue two ⅜-inch (1cm) stars to each shoulder.

7. Using beading needle and black ribbon, work three Straight Stitches on bib, threading two beads on each stitch where indicated before completing stitch. Glue bib to body front.

8. Matching red stars, place hat bill on head front. Place ends of chin strap under bill, making sure strap is centered on face. Glue bill and strap in place, glue one ⅜-inch (1cm) star at each red star on bill. Glue 1-inch (2.5cm) star to center front of hat.

9. Glue cabochons to face for eyes where indicated on graph. Use cotton swab to apply small amount of blush to cheeks. ❦

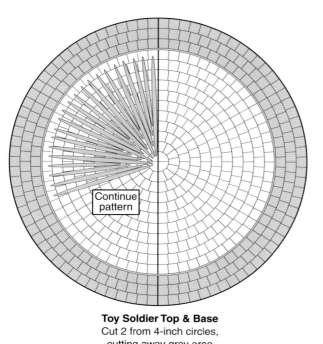

Toy Soldier Top & Base
Cut 2 from 4-inch circles,
cutting away gray area
Stitch top as graphed
Do not stitch base

COLOR KEY

Yards	Worsted Weight Yarn
110 (100.6m)	☐ Bluebird #9822
10 (9.2m)	Uncoded areas on face and neck are Aran #313 Continental Stitches
	⁄ Aran #313 Whipstitch
20 (18.3m)	⁄ Linen #330 Straight Stitch and Whipstitch
	1/8-Inch Ribbon
8 (7.4m)	☐ Silver #001 (2 strands)
50 (45.7m)	■ Black hi lustre #005HL
	⁄ Silver #001 (1-strand) Straight Stitch
	✔ Black hi lustre #005HL Backstitch and Straight Stitch
	○ Attach silver bead
	● Attach black cabochon
	★ Attach 3/8-inch (1cm) silver star

Color numbers given are for Coats & Clark Red Heart Plush worsted weight yarn Art. E719 and Super Saver worsted weight yarn Art. E300, and Kreinik 1/8-inch Ribbon.

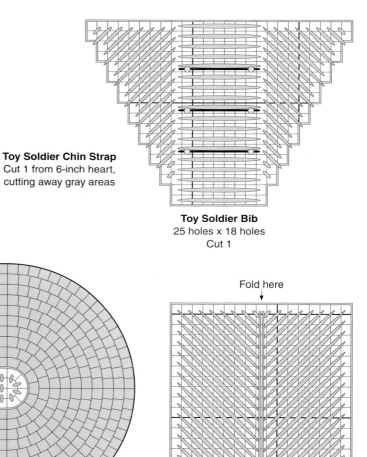

Toy Soldier Bib
25 holes x 18 holes
Cut 1

Toy Soldier Chin Strap
Cut 1 from 6-inch heart,
cutting away gray areas

Toy Soldier Shoulders
Cut 2 from 6-inch heart,
cutting away gray areas

Fold here

Toy Soldier Arm
17 holes x 21 holes
Cut 2

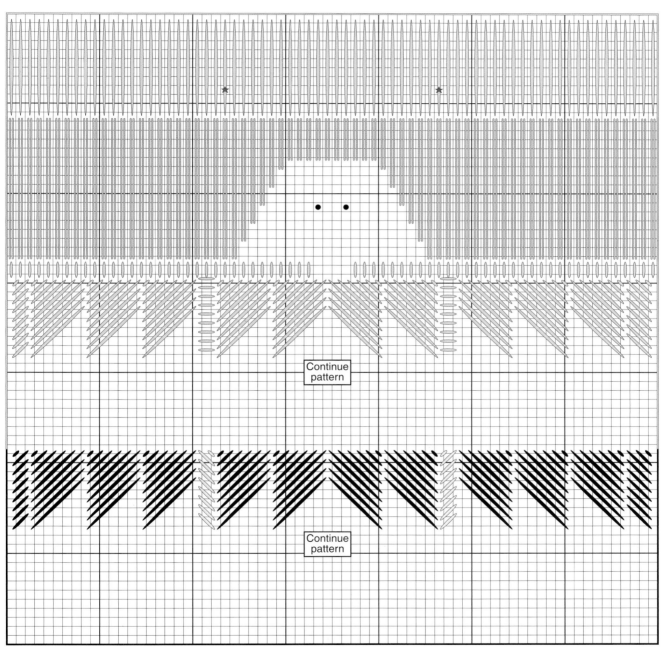

Toy Soldier Body
70 holes x 70 holes
Cut 1

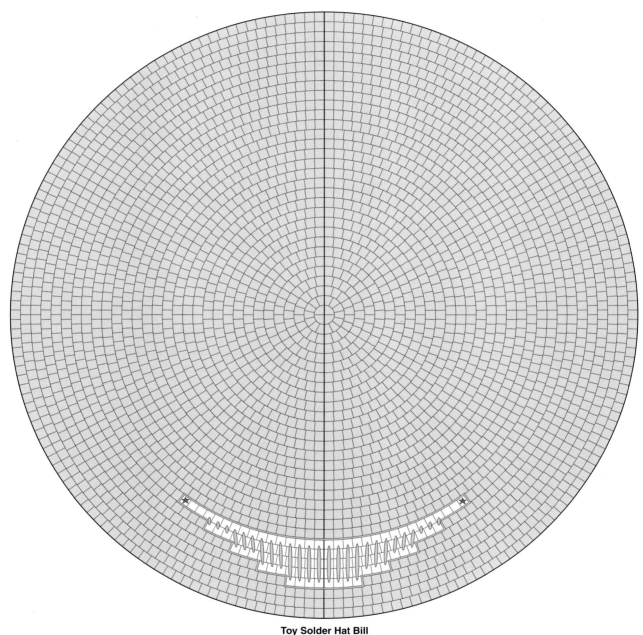

Toy Solder Hat Bill
Cut 1 from 9-inch radial circle,
cutting away gray area

Holiday Advent Dazzler

Bright jewels mark the days on this unique take on the traditional Advent calendar. Add a stone-embellished brad each day for your seasonal countdown.

DESIGN BY MARY T. COSGROVE

Skill Level
Intermediate

Size
10¾ inches W x 13¾ inches H (27.3cm x 34.9cm), excluding hanger

Materials
- 1 sheet 7-count plastic canvas
- Uniek Needloft plastic canvas yarn as listed in color key
- Uniek Needloft metallic craft cord as listed in color key
- #16 tapestry needle
- 1½ yards (1.4m) fine gold metallic braid
- 12 inches (30.5cm) 24-gauge metallic gold craft wire
- 22 (6mm) round gold metallic beads
- 16mm red heart-shaped acrylic faceted stone
- 9mm round acrylic faceted stones
    - 4 topaz
    - 10 ruby
    - 12 turquoise
- ½-inch (1.3cm) flower brads
    - 6 blue
    - 8 deep pink
    - 13 yellow
- Craft stick
- Fast-grab glue

Instructions
1. Cut plastic canvas according to graph (page 140).
2. Stitch and Overcast piece following graph, working uncoded areas with Continental Stitches as follows: white background with Christmas green, blue background with turquoise, pink background with watermelon, yellow background with yellow, peach background with gold.
3. When background stitching is completed, work Backstitches around gift packages and ornaments and Backstitch bows on packages.

Backstitch and Straight Stitch numbers where indicated on packages, ornaments and yellow balls for the first 24 days of December.
4. Using fine gold metallic braid, attach gold beads to tree where indicated.
5. For hanger, thread one end of craft wire through star at top of tree where indicated, wrapping end around wire above edge of canvas to secure. Wrap wire around craft stick to coil. Attach remaining end of wire to other side of star where indicated.

6. Glue faceted stones and heart to flower brads as desired. Allow to dry. As each day of Advent arrives, thread prongs of brads through holes of canvas over numbers, then separate and fold prongs to back of canvas. 🍃

COLOR KEY	
Yards	**Plastic Canvas Yarn**
2 (1.9m)	■ Cinnamon #14
4 (3.7m)	☐ White #41
5 (4.6m)	☐ Turquoise #54
7 (6.5m)	☐ Watermelon #55
15 (13.8m)	☐ Yellow #57
39 (35.7m)	Uncoded areas on white background are Christmas green #28 Continental Stitches
	Uncoded areas on blue background are turquoise #54 Continental Stitches
	Uncoded areas on pink background are watermelon #55 Continental Stitches
	Uncoded areas on yellow background are yellow #57 Continental Stitches
	⁄ Christmas green #28 Overcast
	⁄ Turquoise #54 Backstitch and Straight Stitch
	⁄ Watermelon #55 Backstitch and Straight Stitch
	⁄ Yellow #57 Backstitch and Straight Stitch
	Metallic Craft Cord
7 (6.5m)	Uncoded areas on peach background are gold #55001 Continental Stitches
	⁄ Gold #55001 Overcast
	⦿ Attach gold bead
	● Attach wire hanger
Color numbers given are for Uniek Needloft plastic canvas yarn and metallic craft cord.	

Holiday Advent Dazzler Tree
70 holes x 90 holes
Cut 1

Polar Love

Cute and cuddly, these plastic canvas polar bears are right at home on a painted board that mimics an icy habitat.

DESIGN BY LEE LINDEMAN

Skill Level
Intermediate

Size
12½ inches W x 4¾ inches H x 9½ inches D (31.8cm x 12.1cm x 24.1cm)

Materials
- 1½ sheets 7-count plastic canvas
- Uniek Needloft plastic canvas yarn as listed in color key
- 6-strand embroidery floss as listed in color key
- #16 tapestry needle
- Small amount white craft foam
- Small amount plastic foam
- Clear glitter
- 9 x 12-inch (22.9 x 30.5cm) wood plaque
- 7 (7mm) round foil-backed light sapphire or crystal transparent cabochons
- Acrylic paint: light blue, medium blue and white
- Paintbrushes
- Clear protective spray
- Polyester fiberfill
- 12¼ x 9¼-inch piece felt in desired color
- Clear tacky glue
- Hot-glue gun

Preparation
1. Cut plastic canvas according to graphs (this page and page 144).
2. Cut two small bear ears and two large bear ears from craft foam using patterns given.
3. Paint sides and top of plaque with light blue. Before paint dries, use dry brush to swirl medium blue and white on top to get a water-like effect. Allow to dry thoroughly.
4. Spray painted areas of plaque with clear protective coat. Allow to dry thoroughly. Glue felt to bottom of plaque.

Stitching
1. Stitch and Overcast large and small ice floes. Stitch tall iceberg and bear pieces, reversing the following

**Polar Love
Small Bear Ear**
Cut 2 from
white craft foam

**Polar Love
Large Bear Ear**
Cut 2 from
white craft foam

COLOR KEY	
Yards	**Plastic Canvas Yarn**
75 (68.6m)	☐ White #41
1 (1m)	✏ Black #00 Whipstitch
	6-Strand Embroidery Floss
1 (1m)	✏ Black (6-ply) Straight Stitch
	● Black (3-ply) French Knot
	✏ Attach ear
Color numbers given are for Uniek Needloft plastic canvas yarn.	

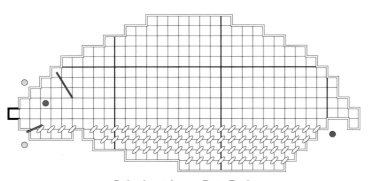

Polar Love Large Bear Body
33 holes x 15 holes
Cut 2, reverse 1

before stitching: one tall iceberg side, one large bear body, two each of large bear legs, one small bear body and two each of small bear legs.

2. When background stitching is completed, work black floss French Knots for eyes with 3 plies of yarn.

3. Whipstitch jagged edges of iceberg sides together from dot to dot, then Whipstitch end to sides between brackets. Overcast bottom edges. Fill iceberg with fiberfill.

4. Whipstitch corresponding body pieces together along head edges from yellow dot to yellow dot,

Whipstitching nose area with black yarn. Use black floss to work mouth over edge where indicated.

5. Whipstitch remaining edges of small bear body pieces together, filling with fiberfill before closing.

6. Whipstitch large bear body pieces together from top yellow dot, over back and around tail to red dot. Whipstitch gusset in place along bottom edges from bottom yellow dot to red dot, filling with fiberfill before closing.

7. Matching edges, Whipstitch corresponding leg pieces together, filling each with small amounts of fiberfill.

8. Using photo as a guide, hot glue

legs to bears. Glue ears to heads where indicated on graphs.

Finishing

1. Spread small amount of clear glue along edges of ice floes and sprinkle glitter over moist glue. Allow to dry. Shake off excess glitter.

2. Using photo as a guide through step 4, hot-glue ice floes and iceberg to plaque top. Glue polar bears to large ice floe.

3. For snowballs, press plastic foam into several ½-inch balls; glue to large ice floe.

4. Glue cabochons to plaque for water droplets. 🌿

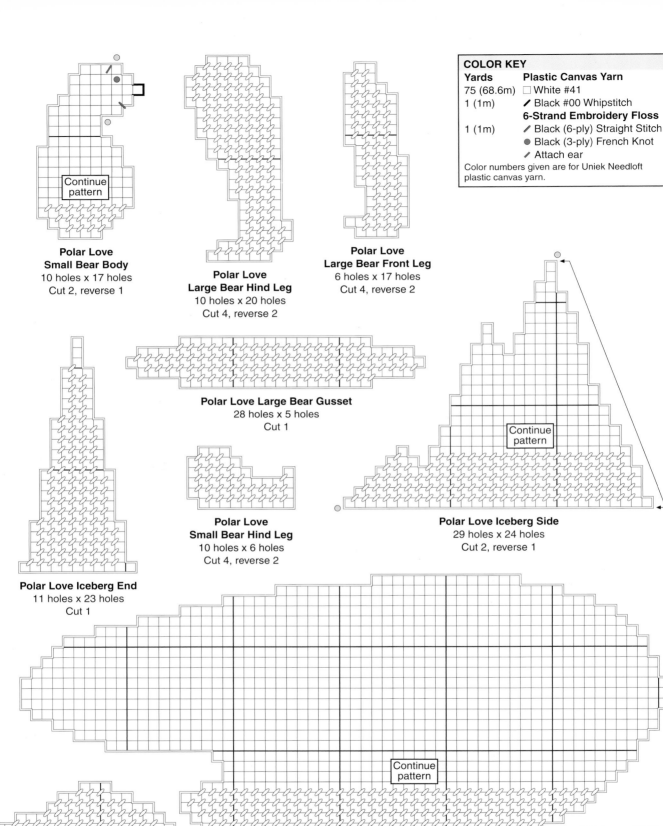

COLOR KEY

Yards	Plastic Canvas Yarn
75 (68.6m)	☐ White #41
1 (1m)	✎ Black #00 Whipstitch
	6-Strand Embroidery Floss
1 (1m)	✎ Black (6-ply) Straight Stitch
	● Black (3-ply) French Knot
	✎ Attach ear

Color numbers given are for Uniek Needloft plastic canvas yarn.

**Polar Love
Small Bear Body**
10 holes x 17 holes
Cut 2, reverse 1

**Polar Love
Large Bear Hind Leg**
10 holes x 20 holes
Cut 4, reverse 2

**Polar Love
Large Bear Front Leg**
6 holes x 17 holes
Cut 4, reverse 2

Polar Love Large Bear Gusset
28 holes x 5 holes
Cut 1

**Polar Love
Small Bear Hind Leg**
10 holes x 6 holes
Cut 4, reverse 2

Polar Love Iceberg Side
29 holes x 24 holes
Cut 2, reverse 1

Polar Love Iceberg End
11 holes x 23 holes
Cut 1

Polar Love Large Ice Floe
61 holes x 27 holes
Cut 1

Small Ice Floe
17 holes x 9 holes
Cut 1

**Polar Love
Small Bear Front Leg**
8 holes x 3 holes
Cut 4, reverse 2

Charming Plaid

Classic country style abounds in this darling set that features a gift bag, decorative angel and garland. Strips of plaid fabric and strands of twine are an added decorative touch.

DESIGNS BY TERRY RICIOLI

Skill Level
Beginner

Size
Angel: 5 inches W x 8½ inches H (12.7cm x 21.6cm), excluding halo

Garland: Approximately 29½ inches L x 10 inches H (74.9cm x 25.4cm), including fabric ties

Gift Bag: 4¼ inches W x 5 inches H x 1⅝ inches D (10.8cm x 12.7cm x 4.1cm), excluding handles

Materials
- 2 sheets clear 7-count plastic canvas
- 1 sheet tan 7-count plastic canvas
- ½ sheet each 7-count plastic canvas in rose and light green
- Uniek Needloft plastic canvas yarn as listed in color key
- #16 tapestry needle
- 4 yards (3.7m) hemp twine
- ¼ yard (0.2m) burgundy, tan and green plaid woven cotton fabric
- 11 or 12 mm wood beads
    32 natural
    20 dark brown
- Hot-glue gun

Cutting
1. Cut angel, arms, wings, one small star, two large stars, two hearts and three Christmas trees from clear plastic canvas according to graphs (pages 146 and 148).
2. Cut gift bag front and back from tan plastic canvas according to graph (page 148). Also cut two 10-hole x 33-hole pieces for bag sides and one 27-hole x 10-hole piece for bag base from tan plastic canvas. Bag pieces will remain unstitched.
3. For backing, cut two large stars from tan plastic canvas, two hearts from rose plastic canvas and two trees from light green plastic canvas. Backing pieces will remain unstitched.
4. From plaid fabric, cut or tear 26 (1½ x 5½-inch/3.8 x 14cm) strips.

Stitching
1. Stitch pieces following graphs, reversing one arm before stitching and working uncoded areas with camel Continental Stitches.
2. Overcast angel, arms, wings,

small star and one large tree, which will be used on the gift bag.
3. For garland, Whipstitch hearts, large stars and two Christmas trees to unstitched backing.

Angel Assembly
1. Using photo as a guide throughout assembly, glue wings to back of angel and arms to front.
2. Cut a 5-inch (12.7cm) length of twine for small star hanger and attach to top hole with a Lark's Head Knot. Tie ends together in a knot and place over hands. Glue in place behind hands.
3. For halo, cut 12-inch (30.5cm) length of twine. Loop into a circle three times, placing ends together and trimming any excess. Glue halo and ends to back of head.
4. For angel hanger, cut a 3-inch (7.6cm) length of twine. Tie ends together in a loop. Center and glue knotted end to back of angel at wings and head.

Gift Bag Assembly
1. Using cinnamon yarn, Whipstitch bag front and back to sides, then Whipstitch front, back and sides to base. Do not Overcast top edges.
2. Center and glue unbacked Christmas tree to bag front.

3. For handles, cut four 12-inch (30.5cm) lengths of twine. Place two lengths together as one; tie one end in a knot, leaving about a 1½-inch (3.8cm) tail. If twine is thin, knot twice. Thread on one natural and one dark brown bead; knot again.

4. Thread other end from front to back though bag front where indicated on one side. Knot twice randomly in center of handle, then thread end from back to front through hole indicated on other side of front. Knot on outside of bag, add one dark brown then one natural bead and knot again.

5. Repeat steps 3 and 4 for handle on bag back. Tie five fabric strips to handles.

Garland Assembly

1. For hangers, cut six 6-inch (15.2cm) lengths twine. Attach one length each to hearts, large stars and remaining trees with a Lark's Head Knot.

2. Cut a 1 yard (1m) length of twine. Fold one end over and tie a knot (double knot if twine is thin), leaving about a 1-inch (2.5cm) loop on end.

3. From other end, thread on two dark brown beads, then one natural bead to knot of loop. Tie on one fabric strip, then thread on one natural bead, add another strip, one natural bead, one strip, one natural bead and two dark brown beads.

4. Continue with one natural bead, one strip, one natural bead, one strip, one natural bead, one strip, one natural bead and two dark brown beads.

5. Repeat pattern in step 4 five more times, ending with two dark brown beads.

6. Tie a 1-inch (2.5cm) loop next to last brown bead. Cut excess twine.

7. Using photo as a guide for placement, tie three different ornaments on garland, then repeat ornament pattern. 🌿

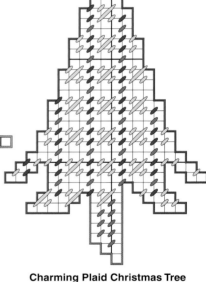

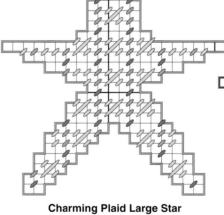

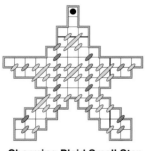

Charming Plaid Christmas Tree
19 holes x 30 holes
Cut 2 from clear
stitch as graphed
Cut 2 from light green
Do not stitch

Charming Plaid Large Star
21 holes x 23 holes
Cut 2 from clear
stitch as graphed
Cut 2 from tan
Do not stitch

Charming Plaid Small Star
13 holes x 13 holes
Cut 1 from clear

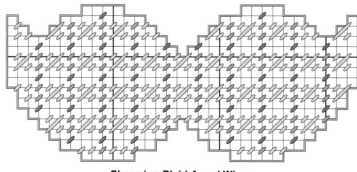

Charming Plaid Angel Wings
33 holes x 15 holes
Cut 1 from clear

COLOR KEY	
Yards	**Plastic Canvas Yarn**
20 (18.3m)	■ Burgundy #03
12 (11m)	□ Lavender #05
12 (11m)	▨ Pumpkin #12
20 (18.3m)	■ Cinnamon #14
10 (9.2m)	■ Forest #29
8 (7.4m)	□ Mermaid #53
12 (11m)	□ Yellow #57
20 (18.3m)	Uncoded areas are camel #43 Continental Stitches
	⁄ Camel #43 Overcast
	● Attach twine handle
	● Attach twine hanger

Color numbers given are for Uniek Needloft plastic canvas yarn.

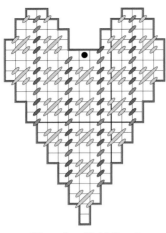

Charming Plaid Heart
15 holes x 21 holes
Cut 2 from clear
stitch as graphed
Cut 2 from rose
Do not stitch

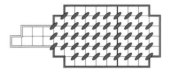

Charming Plaid Angel Arm
14 holes x 6 holes
Cut 2, reverse 1, from clear

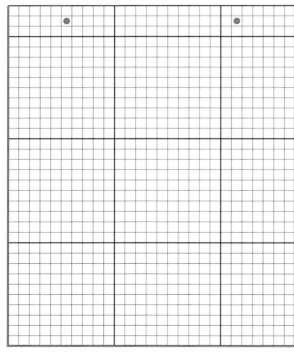

**Charming Plaid
Gift Bag Front & Back**
27 holes x 33 holes
Cut 2 from tan
Do not stitch

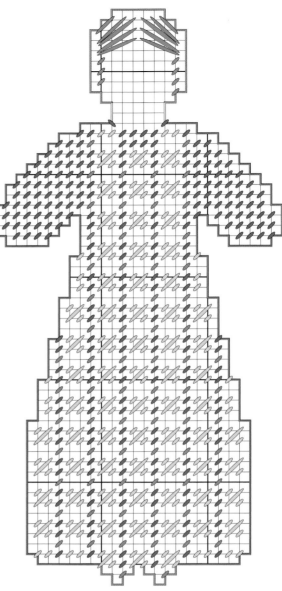

Charming Plaid Angel
27 holes x 56 holes
Cut 1 from clear

COLOR KEY	
Yards	**Plastic Canvas Yarn**
20 (18.3m)	■ Burgundy #03
12 (11m)	□ Lavender #05
12 (11m)	▨ Pumpkin #12
20 (18.3m)	▦ Cinnamon #14
10 (9.2m)	■ Forest #29
8 (7.4m)	▨ Mermaid #53
12 (11m)	□ Yellow #57
20 (18.3m)	Uncoded areas are camel #43 Continental Stitches
	╱ Camel #43 Overcast
	● Attach twine handle
	● Attach twine hanger

Color numbers given are for Uniek Needloft plastic canvas yarn.

Noel Coaster Set

Funky metallic cord and shiny sequin accents combine for a contemporary coaster set that will please even teens.

DESIGN BY MARY T. COSGROVE

Skill Level
Beginner

Size
Coasters: 4½ inches square (11.4cm)

Holder: 4¾ inches W x 2⅛ inches H x 1¾ inches D (12.1cm x 5.4cm x 4.4cm)

Materials
- 1½ sheet 7-count plastic canvas
- Uniek Needloft plastic canvas yarn as listed in color key
- Uniek Needloft metallic craft cord as listed in color key
- Kreinik Fine (#8) Braid as listed in color key
- #16 tapestry needle
- #24 tapestry needle
- 1 sheet 14-count gold metallic perforated paper
- 28 (2–2.5mm) gold metallic beads
- 16 each 4mm metallic beads: red and purple
- Fabric glue

Instructions

1. Cut plastic canvas according to graphs (pages 150 and 151). Cut gold metallic perforated paper to fit coasters.

2. Stitch pieces following graphs, working uncoded areas with white Continental Stitches. Overcast coasters and top edges of holder front, back and sides.

3. When background stitching is completed, work white Backstitches between letters on coasters.

4. Work fine (#8) braid embroidery, stitching holder front as graphed. Stitch holder back, replacing purple hi lustre braid with red hi luster braid. When working long Straight Stitches on coasters and holder pieces, make an additional stitch at end of stitch to add gold bead where indicated.

5. Attach purple beads where indicated with purple hi lustre braid and red beads where indicated with red hi lustre braid.

6. Using Christmas green, Whipstitch holder front and back to holder sides, then Whipstitch holder front, back and sides to base.

7. Glue white side of perforated paper to backs of coasters. Allow to dry. 🍃

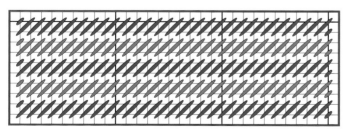

Noel Coaster Holder Base
31 holes x 11 holes
Cut 1

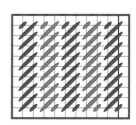

Noel Coaster Holder Side
11 holes x 10 holes
Cut 2

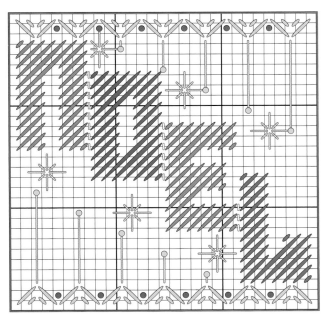

Noel Coaster A
29 holes x 29 holes
Cut 2

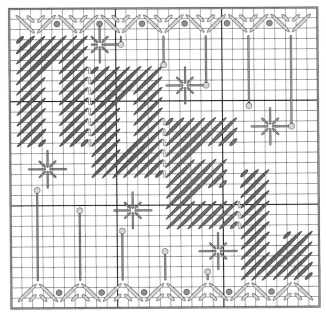

Noel Coaster Holder Front & Back
31 holes x 13 holes
Cut 2
Stitch front as graphed
Stitch back replacing
purple hi lustre with red hi lustre
and purple beads with red beads

Noel Coaster B
29 holes x 29 holes
Cut 2

COLOR KEY

Yards	Plastic Canvas Yarn
14 (12.9m)	■ Christmas red #02
12 (11m)	■ Christmas green #28
11 (10.1m)	■ Bright purple #64
42 (38.4m)	Uncoded areas are white #41 Continental Stitches
	⁄ White #41 Backstitch
	Metallic Craft Cord
8 (7.4m)	□ Gold #55001
	Fine (#8) Braid
6 (5.5m)	⁄ Red hi lustre #003HL Straight Stitch
6 (5.5m)	⁄ Purple hi lustre #012HL Straight Stitch
	○ Attach gold bead
	● Attach red bead
	● Attach purple bead

Color numbers given are for Uniek Needloft
plastic canvas yarn and metallic craft cord
and Kreinik Fine (#8) Braid.

Napkin Wreath

An elegant holiday soiree just isn't the same without a fancy table setting. Dress your napkins up by adding a festive wreath that doubles as a napkin holder.

DESIGN BY ALIDA MACOR

Skill Level
Beginner

Size
3¼ inches in diameter

Materials
- Small amount 7-count plastic canvas
- Uniek Needloft plastic canvas yarn as listed in color key
- #16 tapestry needle
- 9 inches (22.9cm) ⅛-inch/ 3mm-wide satin ribbon in color desired
- 6 (5mm) round gold metallic beads
- Hand-sewing needle
- Green sewing thread

Instructions
1. Cut plastic canvas according to graph.
2. Stitch and Overcast piece following graph.
3. Using hand-sewing needle and green thread through step 4, attach beads to wreath where indicated on graph.
4. Tie ribbon in a bow and tack to top center of wreath as indicated on graph.

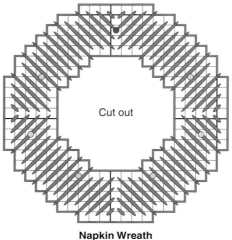

Napkin Wreath
21 holes x 21 holes
Cut 1

COLOR KEY	
Yards	**Plastic Canvas Yarn**
3 (2.8m)	■ Christmas green #28
	○ Attach gold bead
	● Attach ribbon bow

Color numbers given are for Uniek Needloft plastic canvas yarn.

Peace Messenger

Bringing a message of peace, this dove will add a serene feeling of love to your home year round.

DESIGN BY KATHY WIRTH

Skill Level
Intermediate

Size
10½ inches W x 19¾ inches H (26.7cm x 50.2cm)

Materials
- 1½ sheets 7-count plastic canvas
- Worsted weight yarn as listed in color key
- 4mm Rainbow Gallery Plastic Canvas 7 Metallic Needlepoint Yarn as listed in color key
- 6-strand embroidery floss as listed in color key
- #16 tapestry needle
- Small amount fiberfill
- ½ yard (0.5m) ⅝-inch/1.6cm-wide sheer white ribbon
- 24 inches (61cm) 24-gauge silver wire
- 7 (½-inch/13mm) white iridescent pompoms
- 12 inches (30.5cm) ³⁄₁₆-inch (0.5cm) dowel
- 5 x 2¼-inch large clown head #84927 wood tassel top from Toner Plastics
- White acrylic paint
- Sand paper
- Paintbrush
- Small pliers
- Pencil
- Hot-glue gun

Project Note
Keep metallic needlepoint yarn smooth and flat while stitching.

Instructions
1. Cut plastic canvas according to graphs (page 154).
2. Lightly sand tassel top (base) and dowel; wipe clean. Paint each with white acrylic paint. Allow to dry.
3. Stitch signs following graphs, working uncoded background with white Continental Stitches. Stitch remaining pieces, reversing one dove and two wings before stitching, then working stitches in reverse. Leave portion indicated on doves unstitched.
4. When background stitching is completed, use black floss to work lettering, beaks and eyes.
5. Whipstitch wrong sides of sign pieces together with silver.
6. Overcast bottom edges of dove pieces between dots, then Whipstitch pieces together with silver at beak area, working a black stitch over edge where indicated. Whipstitch remaining edges together with white pearl, stuffing lightly with fiberfill while Whipstitching.
7. Matching edges, Whipstitch wrong sides of two wings together. Repeat for remaining wings. Glue wings to body as in photo.

Assembly
1. Glue pompoms to base as in photo.
2. Run wire through beak and back through again to secure, leaving about a 2-inch (5.1cm) tail.
3. Thread other end of wire through needle and run through sign from top to bottom where indicated with arrows, using small pliers to pull through. Leave approximately 4 inches (10.2cm) between beak and sign. Curl wire around pencil above and below beak and below sign. Trim ends as desired.
4. Push one end of dowel through hole in base as far as desired. Turn base upside down and drip hot glue inside to secure dowel. Place hot glue on other end of dowel and insert several inches (centimeters) through opening in bottom of body.
5. Wrap ribbon around dowel at top of base and tie in bow. Glue to secure. 🦋

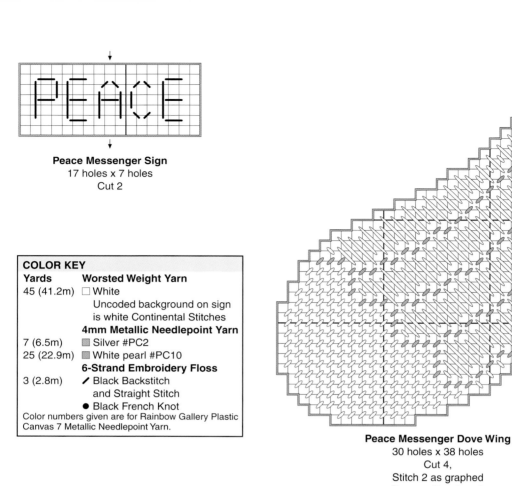

Peace Messenger Sign
17 holes x 7 holes
Cut 2

COLOR KEY

Yards	Worsted Weight Yarn
45 (41.2m)	☐ White
	Uncoded background on sign
	is white Continental Stitches
	4mm Metallic Needlepoint Yarn
7 (6.5m)	▨ Silver #PC2
25 (22.9m)	▨ White pearl #PC10
	6-Strand Embroidery Floss
3 (2.8m)	✁ Black Backstitch
	and Straight Stitch
	● Black French Knot

Color numbers given are for Rainbow Gallery Plastic
Canvas 7 Metallic Needlepoint Yarn.

Peace Messenger Dove Wing
30 holes x 38 holes
Cut 4,
Stitch 2 as graphed
Reverse 2 and work
stitches in reverse

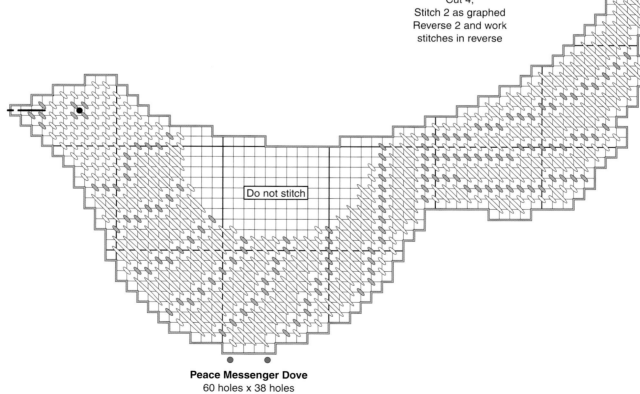

Do not stitch

Peace Messenger Dove
60 holes x 38 holes
Cut 2,
Stitch 1 as graphed
Reverse 1 and work
stitches in reverse

Christmas Cross

Rhinestones add a little brilliance to this handsome cross that will become the focal point of your holiday decor.

DESIGN BY RONDA BRYCE

Skill Level
Beginner

Size
10½ inches W x 13¼ inches H
(26.7cm x 33.7cm)

Materials
- 1 sheet 7-count plastic canvas
- Uniek Needloft plastic canvas yarn as listed in color key
- #16 tapestry needle
- 3 (13mm) round red transparent acrylic faceted stones
- 12mm silver toggle ring
- Hand-sewing needle
- Black sewing thread
- Jewel glue

Instructions
1. Cut plastic canvas according to graph.
2. Stitch and Overcast cross following graph, working un-coded areas with Christmas red Continental Stitches.
3. Using black thread, attach toggle ring to center top edge.
4. Using photo as a guide, glue red acrylic stones to center of cross bar. Allow to dry. 🌿

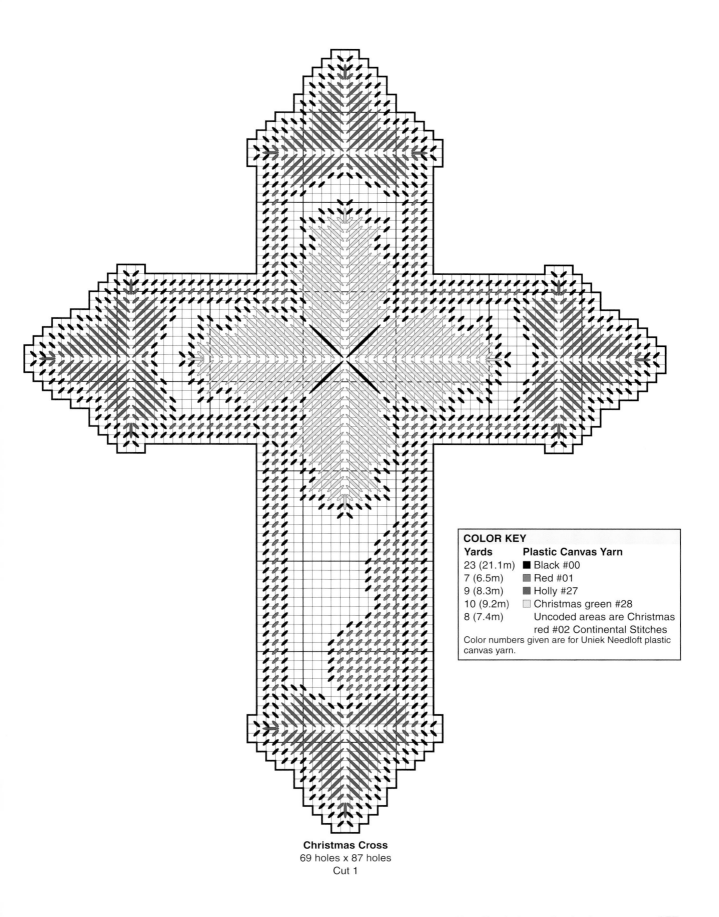

COLOR KEY

Yards	Plastic Canvas Yarn
23 (21.1m)	■ Black #00
7 (6.5m)	▨ Red #01
9 (8.3m)	▨ Holly #27
10 (9.2m)	▢ Christmas green #28
8 (7.4m)	Uncoded areas are Christmas red #02 Continental Stitches

Color numbers given are for Uniek Needloft plastic canvas yarn.

Christmas Cross
69 holes x 87 holes
Cut 1

Quilted Stars Doily

The beauty of quilt blocks comes to life in this classic doily that can be interpreted as festive stars or pretty poinsettias.

DESIGN BY DEBRA ARCH

Skill Level
Intermediate

Size
12¼ inches W x 10⅞ inches H
(31.1cm x 27.6cm)

Materials
- 1 artist-size sheet 7-count plastic canvas
- Uniek Needloft plastic canvas yarn as listed in color key
- #16 tapestry needle
- 12-inch (30.5cm) square white felt
- Hot-glue gun

Instructions
1. Cut plastic canvas according to graph.
2. Stitch and Overcast doily following graph, working un-coded areas with Christmas red Continental Stitches.
3. Cut felt to fit doily, glue to back side. 🪡

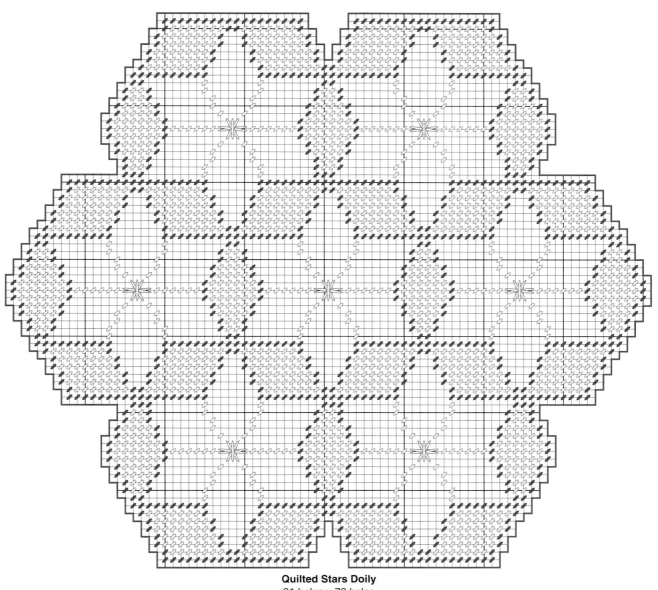

Quilted Stars Doily
81 holes x 72 holes
Cut 1

COLOR KEY	
Yards	**Plastic Canvas Yarn**
2 (1.9m)	☐ Lemon #20
35 (32m)	■ Holly #27
40 (36.6m)	☐ White #41
20 (18.3m)	Uncoded areas are Christmas red #02 Continental Stitches
Color numbers given are for Uniek Needloft plastic canvas yarn.	

Joy to the World

Your holiday spirit will shine for all to see when you display this bright, contemporary wall hanging.

DESIGN BY MARY T. COSGROVE

Skill Level
Advanced

Size
10⅝ inches W x 12¾ inches H (27cm x 32.4cm), excluding hanger and ribbon tails

Materials
- 1 sheet 7-count plastic canvas
- Coats & Clark Red Heart Classic worsted weight yarn Art. E267 as listed in color key
- Coats & Clark Red Heart Super Saver worsted weight yarn Art. E300 as listed in color key
- Coats & Clark Red Heart Kids worsted weight yarn Art. E711 as listed in color key
- #16 tapestry needle
- 7 (¾-inch/19mm) gold jingle bells
- 10 (8mm) gold metallic beads
- 1 (10mm) gold metallic bead
- 54 inches (139.7cm) ¼-inch/7mm-wide red satin ribbon
- Dry-erase marker

Project Note
Because of the many complex areas to be cut out in the center of this wall hanging, marking all edges with a dry-erase marker before cutting is recommended. Rub markings off with cloth or wash off with water and dry thoroughly.

Instructions
1. Cut plastic canvas according to graph (page 162), cutting out white areas in center.

2. Cut red satin ribbon for bell tails as follows: two 6-inch (15.2cm) lengths, two 7-inch (17.8cm) lengths, two 8-inch (20.3cm) lengths, one 9-inch (22.9cm) length. Cut one 4-inch (10.2cm) length red ribbon for hanger.

3. Stitch and Overcast piece following graph, working uncoded areas with Continental Stitches as follows: lavender background with orchid, pink background with grenadine and white background with lime.

4. Using yellow yarn, attach gold beads to the center of star with 10mm bead in center, two 8mm beads on top and sides and four 8mm beads on bottom.

5. For bell tails, thread lengths of red ribbon from front to back through holes indicated; knot securely on back side. Attach bells to other ends.

6. At arrows along top edge, thread ends of hanger ribbon through yarn on back of piece, knotting ends to secure. 🪻

COLOR KEY

Yards	Worsted Weight Yarn
8 (7.4m)	☐ Parakeet #513
6 (5.5m)	☐ Orchid #530
4 (3.7m)	☐ Grenadine #730
7 (6.5m)	■ Cherry red #912
6 (5.5m)	☐ Yellow #2230
	Uncoded areas on lavender background are orchid #530 Continental Stitches
	Uncoded areas on pink background are grenadine #730 Continental Stitches
26 (23.8m)	Uncoded areas on white background are lime #2652 Continental Stitches
	✎ Lime #2652 Overcast
	— Attach 8mm gold bead
	▬ Attach 10mm gold bead
	● Attach 6-inch (15.2cm) red ribbon
	● Attach 7-inch (17.8cm) red ribbon
	● Attach 8-inch (20.3cm) red ribbon
	○ Attach 9-inch (22.9cm) red ribbon

Color numbers given are for Coats & Clark Red Heart Classic worsted weight yarn Art. E267, Super Saver worsted weight yarn Art. E300 and Kids worsted weight yarn Art. E711.

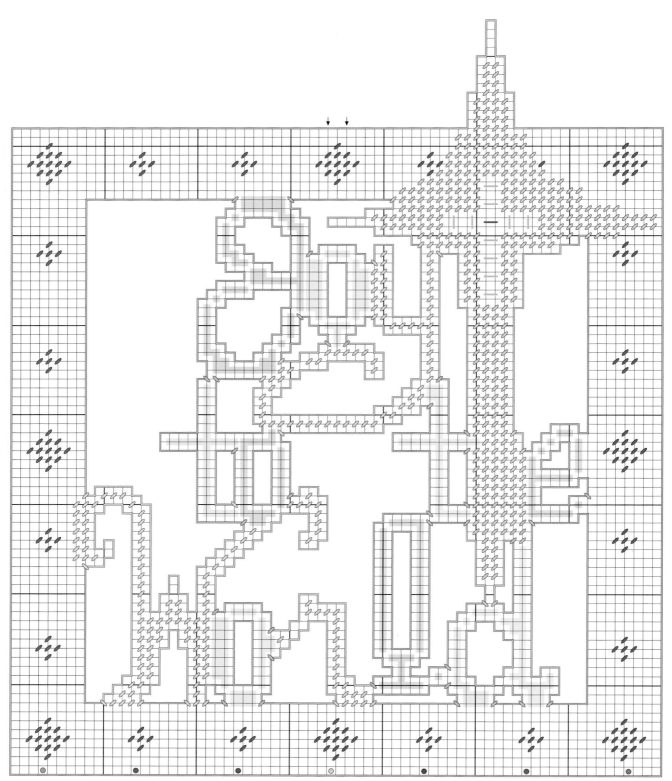

Joy to the World
70 holes x 84 holes
Cut 1

Star Votive Holder

Beads and iridescent yarn sparkle and shine with a brightness that will upstage even the brightest star. Add a votive candle for a cheery addition to any room.

DESIGN BY TERRY RICIOLI

Skill Level
Intermediate

Size
4¾ inches H x 7¼ inches in diameter (12.1cm x 18.4cm)

Materials
- 4 (5-inch) Uniek QuickShape plastic canvas stars
- Uniek Needloft iridescent craft cord as listed in color key
- #16 tapestry needle
- 12 (10mm) gold jump rings
- 12 (2-inch/5.1cm) head pins
- 20 (12mm) transparent crystal star beads
- Approximately 84 silver-lined E beads
- Needle-nose pliers
- Round-nose pliers
- Wire cutters

Project Note
This votive holder will fit a 4-inch (10.2cm) diameter candle jar.

Please use caution. Plastic canvas and plastic canvas yarn will melt and burn if they get too hot or come in contact with a flame. Never leave a lighted candle unattended. Recommended for decorative purposes only.

Instructions
1. Cut stars according to graph (page 172), cutting away gray areas.
2. Stitch and Overcast stars following graph, keeping stitching on back sides as neat as possible.
3. To connect stars, open eight jump rings and attach stars at points where indicated on graphs, forming a circle. Close jump rings.
4. For short dangles, using wire cutters, trim ⅜-inch (1cm) from four head pins. String E beads and one star bead on each short dangle, varying order and leaving ⅜-inch (1cm) on end. Bend this end in a loop. Set aside.
5. For each of the remaining eight long dangles, string E beads and two star beads, varying order and leaving ⅜-inch (1cm) on end. Bend this end in a loop.
6. For dangles in center of each star, open loops on one short and one long dangle and attach to jump rings; close loops.
7. Attach remaining long dangles to top connecting jump rings.

GRAPH ON PAGE 172

Angel Bright

Sweet and serene, this pretty angel centerpiece houses a tiny electric candle for a warm holiday glow.

DESIGN BY LAURA VICTORY

Skill Level
Intermediate

Size
13 inches W x 17 inches H x 7½ inches D (33cm x 43.2cm x 19.1cm), including picks and berries

Materials
- 3 sheets 7-count plastic canvas
- Uniek Needloft plastic canvas yarn as listed in color key
- Uniek Needloft solid metallic craft cord as listed in color key
- #16 tapestry needle
- Blush
- 2 (8mm) round black beads
- 25 inches (63.5cm) ½-inch/1.3cm-wide silver sequined trim
- 9 inches (22.9cm) 1-inch/2.5cm-wide frilly silver trim
- Curly doll hair in desired color
- 3 (1-inch/2.5cm) round decorative silver buttons
- 8 x 26-inch (20.3 x 66cm) piece white netting
- 7¾ x 4¾ x 3¾-inch (19.7 x 12.1 x 9.5cm) piece florist's foam
- 9–9¼-inch (22.9–23.5cm) tall single electric clear candle
- 1½-inch (3.8cm) blue candle light bulb
- Metallic silver acrylic paint
- Small paintbrush
- Various Christmas picks and berries in silver, blues and white
- Hand-sewing needle
- Black and white sewing thread
- All-purpose glue
- Hot-glue gun

Project Note
Please use caution when candle is burning. Do not leave unattended.

Instructions
1. Cut plastic canvas according to graphs (pages 166 and 167). Cut one 53-hole x 27-hole piece for base. Base will remain unstitched.
2. Stitch body front, back and sides following graphs. Overcast around side and top edges of head with pale peach and inside edges on body back with white.
3. When background stitching is completed, work burgundy Backstitches on head for mouth. Using hand-sewing needle and black thread, attach beads for eyes where indicated. Apply blush to cheek areas.
4. Using white and beginning from bottom, Whipstitch front to sides. Whipstitch back to sides, then Whipstitch front, back and sides to unstitched base. Using pale peach, Whipstitch bottom edge of head to top edge of front from dot to dot. Overcast all remaining edges with white.

Assembly
1. Using photo as a guide throughout assembly, hot glue hair to head as desired.
2. Fold frilly silver trim in half to a 4½-inch (11.45cm) length. Use hand-sewing needle and white thread to gather and sew around neck for collar. Following graph, attach top button to front with white thread and remaining buttons with white yarn.
3. Using hand-sewing needle and white thread through step 4, sew silver sequin trim around bottom edge of body.
4. Gather netting at center of 8-inch (20.3cm) width, so each wing is about 4 inches (10.15cm) wide. Sew to back of head and neck.
5. Place florist's foam in body for correct position, trimming if necessary to fit. Remove foam and press candle into center top of foam, making an impression. Remove candle and fill impression with all purpose glue; place candle back in impression. Allow to dry.

6. Paint stem of candle with silver metallic paint. Allow to dry. Replace clear bulb with blue bulb.

7. Place foam in body and thread electric cord of candle through hole in back.

8. Arrange Christmas picks and berries in foam as desired, making sure blue light bulb can be seen. ❧

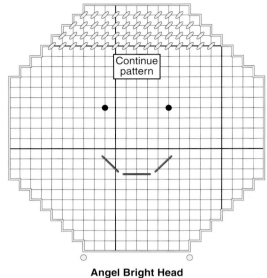

Angel Bright Head
24 holes x 24 holes
Cut 1

COLOR KEY	
Yards	**Plastic Canvas Yarn**
54 (49.4m)	☐ White #41
54 (49.4m)	■ Dark royal #48
9 (8.3m)	☐ Pale peach #56
1 (1m)	✐ Burgundy #03 Backstitch
	Solid Metallic Craft Cord
10 (9.2m)	☐ Solid silver #55021
	● Attach black bead
	● Attach silver button

Color numbers given are for Uniek Needloft plastic canvas yarn and metallic craft cord.

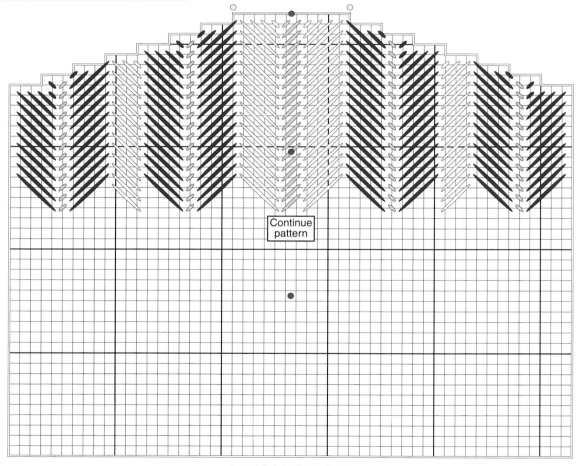

Angel Bright Body Front
53 holes x 43 holes
Cut 1

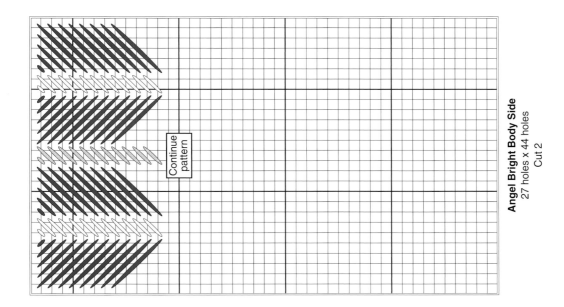

Angel Bright Body Side
27 holes x 44 holes
Cut 2

Continue pattern

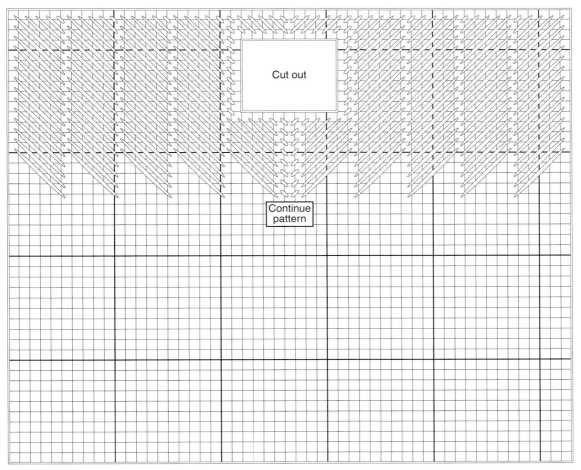

Cut out

Continue pattern

Angel Bright Body Back
53 holes x 44 holes
Cut 1

Joy Wall Hanging

Add a fun and funky touch to your home for the holidays by displaying your joy in the form of a cheery three-piece wall hanging.

DESIGN BY RONDA BRYCE

Skill Level
Beginner

Size
Each Piece: 4½ inches W x 7 inches H (11.4cm x 17.8cm)

Materials
- 1 sheet 7-count plastic canvas
- Uniek Needloft plastic canvas yarn as listed in color key
- ⅛-inch/3mm-wide satin ribbon as listed in color key
- #16 tapestry needle
- Small red ribbon rose
- 9 (6mm) ruby transparent faceted beads
- 6 (⁷⁄₁₆-inch/11mm) burgundy buttons with shanks
- 3 (12mm) silver toggle rings
- 3 (1½-inch/3.8cm) red tassels
- Hand-sewing needle
- Red, white and bright green sewing thread

Instructions
1. Cut plastic canvas according to graphs.

2. Stitch and Overcast pieces following graphs, working uncoded areas on "J" piece with bright green Continental Stitches and uncoded areas on "O" and "Y" pieces with white Continental Stitches.

3. When background stitching is completed, work holly Straight Stitches and Running Stitches and bright green Straight Stitches. Loosely work red ribbon Straight Stitches on "O" piece.

4. On "J" piece, use hand-sewing needle and red thread to stitch three burgundy buttons to center of leaves. Using bright green thread, attach toggle ring to center top edge at arrow and tassel to center bottom edge at arrow.

5. On "O" piece, use hand-sewing needle and red thread to attach red beads where indicated on graph. Make a small bow with red ribbon. Attach bow to bottom of "O" where indicated, then attach red ribbon rose to center of bow.

6. Use white thread to attach toggle ring to center top edge at arrow and tassel to center bottom edge at arrow.

7. On "Y" piece, use hand-sewing needle and red thread to stitch three burgundy buttons to center of leaves. Using white thread, attach toggle ring to center top edge at arrow and tassel to center bottom edge at arrow. 🌿

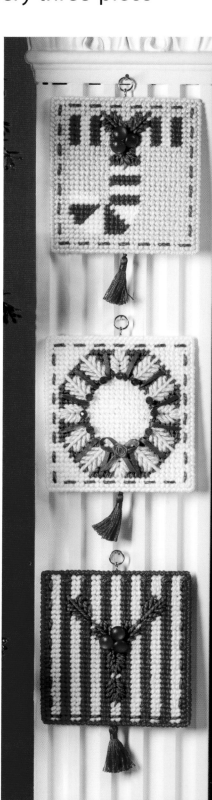

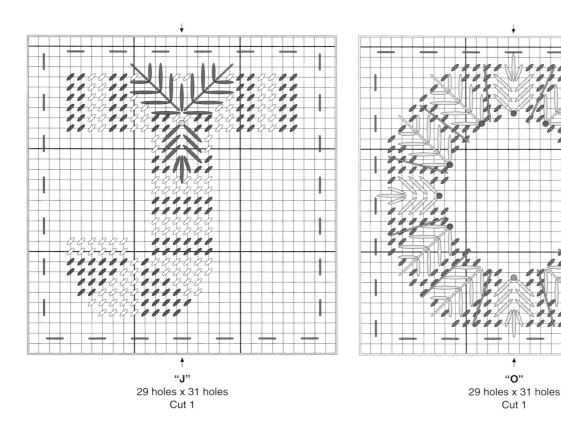

"J"
29 holes x 31 holes
Cut 1

"O"
29 holes x 31 holes
Cut 1

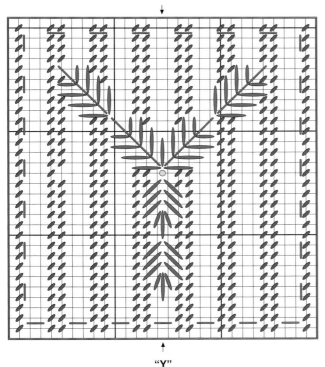

"Y"
29 holes x 31 holes
Cut 1

COLOR KEY	
Yards	**Plastic Canvas Yarn**
14 (12.9m)	■ Red #01
12 (11m)	■ Holly #27
20 (18.3m)	□ White #41
16 (14.7m)	□ Bright green #61
	Uncoded areas on "O" and "Y" pieces are white #41 Continental Stitches
	Uncoded area on "J" piece is bright green #61 Continental Stitches
	╱ Holly #27 Straight Stitch and Running Stitch
	╱ Bright green #61 Straight Stitch
⅛-Inch-Wide Ribbon	
2 (1.9m)	╱ Red Straight Stitch
	● Attach red ribbon bow
	● Attach red bead
	○ Attach 3 burgundy buttons
Color numbers given are for Uniek Needloft plastic canvas yarn.	

Angels Around the World Garland

Celebrate a world of color when you decorate with this festive garland that features loving angels from around the globe.

DESIGN BY GINA WOODS

Skill Level
Intermediate

Size
46¾ inches W x 3⅜ inches H (118.7cm x 8.6cm)

Materials
- ¼ sheet 7-count plastic canvas
- 4 Uniek QuickShape 5-inch plastic canvas hexagons
- 4 Uniek QuickShape 4-inch plastic canvas radial circles
- Worsted weight yarn as listed in color key
- Paton Yarns Brilliant light weight yarn as listed in color key
- #16 tapestry needle
- 8 (6-inch/15.2cm) lengths 20-gauge gold wire
- ⅞-inch (2.2cm) in diameter round object
- Hand-sewing needle
- Sewing thread
- Small wire cutters
- Hot-glue gun

Instructions

1. Cut plastic canvas according to graphs (pages 171 and 172), cutting away gray areas on robes and wings (hexagons) and on connectors (radial circles). **Note:** *Carefully cut apart sections of hexagons so that each section can be used.*

2. Following graphs, stitch and Overcast connectors. When background stitching is completed, work white twinkle Straight Stitches. Stitch wings; do not Overcast.

3. Following graphs and angel color combinations chart throughout, stitch and Overcast heads. Stitch robes; Overcast side edges from red dot to red dot.

4. Using photo as a guide through step 7 and using color combination chart, glue heads to top fronts of robes. Glue wings to backs of robes.

5. For halos, wrap each wire around an object ⅞-inch (2.2cm) in diameter. Wrap end around wire just below circle and leave a 1¼-inch/3.2cm-long tail (see Fig. 1).

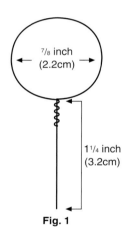

⅞ inch (2.2cm)

1¼ inch (3.2cm)

Fig. 1

6. Place halo behind head and tail behind robe. Using hand-sewing needle and sewing thread, sew to yarn on back sides.

7. To form garland, glue connector ends behind wings. 🍃

ANGEL COLOR COMBINATION CHART

Robe	Skin	Hair
Light blue	Peach	Medium brown
Medium purple	Peach	Dark brown
Medium blue	Light brown	Dark brown
Orchid	Peach	Light terra-cotta
Light blue	Medium brown	Black
Medium purple	Light brown	Black
Medium blue	Peach	Gold
Orchid	Light brown	Black

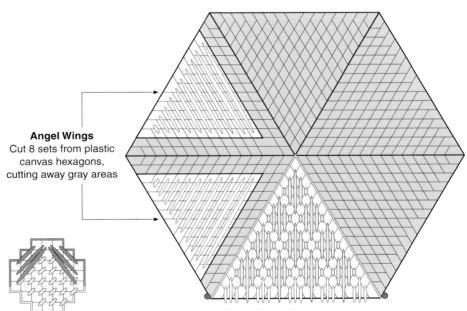

COLOR KEY

Yards	Worsted Weight Yarn
18 (16.5m)	■ Navy
6 (5.5m)	☐ Light blue
6 (5.5m)	Medium blue
6 (5.5m)	Orchid
6 (5.5m)	Medium purple
4 (3.7m)	☐ Peach
3 (2.8m)	Light brown
3 (2.8m)	Black
2 (1.9m)	Dark brown
2 (1.9m)	▨ Medium brown
1 (1m)	Light terra-cotta
1 (1m)	Gold
	Light Weight Yarn
15 (13.8m)	☐ White twinkle #03005
	⁄ White twinkle #03005 Straight Stitch

Color number given is for Patons Yarns
Brilliant light weight yarn.

Angel Wings
Cut 8 sets from plastic
canvas hexagons,
cutting away gray areas

Angel Head
7 holes x 7 holes
Cut 8
Stitch 1 as graphed
Stitch remaining 7, following
color combination chart

Angel Robe
Cut 8 from plastic canvas hexagons,
cutting away gray areas
Stitch 2 as graphed and
2 each, replacing light
blue with medium blue,
medium purple and orchid

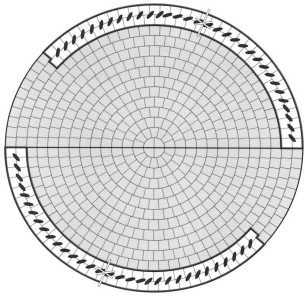

Angel Connector
Cut 7 from 4-inch radial circles,
cutting away gray areas

COLOR KEY	
Yards	**Worsted Weight Yarn**
18 (16.5m)	■ Navy
6 (5.5m)	□ Light blue
6 (5.5m)	Medium blue
6 (5.5m)	Orchid
6 (5.5m)	Medium purple
4 (3.7m)	□ Peach
3 (2.8m)	Light brown
3 (2.8m)	Black
2 (1.9m)	Dark brown
2 (1.9m)	■ Medium brown
1 (1m)	Light terra-cotta
1 (1m)	Gold
	Light Weight Yarn
15 (13.8m)	□ White twinkle #03005
	⁄ White twinkle #03005
	Straight Stitch

Color number given is for Patons Yarns
Brilliant light weight yarn.

Star Votive Holder

CONTINUED FROM PAGE 163

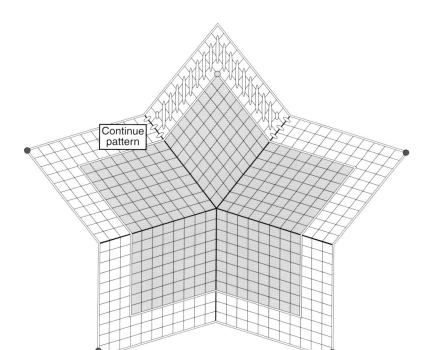

Continue
pattern

Star Votive Holder Star
Cut 4 from plastic canvas star,
cutting away gray area

COLOR KEY	
Yards	**Iridescent Craft Cord**
20 (18.3m)	□ White #55033
	● Attach connecting jump ring
	○ Attach center jump ring

Color numbers given are for Uniek Needloft
iridescent craft cord.

Special Thanks
We would like to acknowledge and thank the following designers whose original work has been published in this collection. We appreciate and value their creativity and dedication to designing quality plastic canvas projects!

Debra Arch
Christmas Cardinal, Chubby Cherubs, Frosteen, Jolly Snowman Canister, Quilted Stars Doily, Reindeer Stocking, Toy Soldier

Angie Arickx
Angel Elegance, Buddy Bears, Festive Fir Tree, O Snowy Night

Ronda Bryce
Christmas Cross, Jolly Time Mug, Joy Wall Hanging, North Pole Pals, Warm Hands Mug

Judy Collishaw
Sweet Treat Pals

Mary T. Cosgrove
Ear Ornaments, Holiday Advent Dazzler, Joy to the World, Kris Kringle Napkin Rings, Noel Coaster Set, Plaid Pleaser, Pocket Packs, Sunbonnet Friends, Sweet Treat Basket

Nancy Dorman
Deck the Halls Snowman, O Tannenbaum

Janelle Giese
Peppermint & Ribbons, Victorian Poinsettia, Wee Country Angels Ornaments & Topper

Mildred E. Goeppel
Feathered Friends

Betty Hansen
Jolly St. Nick, Mini Gift Holders, Treat Mat

Lee Lindeman
Belle, Polar Love, Santa Shelf Sitter

Alida Macor
Floral Beauty, Napkin Wreath

Sandra Miller Maxfield
Holly Jolly Bathroom Tissue Cover

Terry Ricioli
Charming Plaid, Star Votive Holder

Cynthia Roberts
Christmas Cheer, Gift Card Holder, Gift of Joy, Smilin' Snowman

Deborah Scheblein
Santa's Helper

Laura Victory
Angel Bright

Michele Wilcox
Frosty's Winter

Kathy Wirth
Peace Messenger, Santa Triptych

Gina Woods
Angels Around the World Garland, Cookie Cutouts, Holiday Lights, Kaleidoscope Star

Stitch Guide

Use the following diagrams to expand your plastic canvas stitching skills. For each diagram, bring needle up through canvas at the red number one and go back down through the canvas at the red number two. The second stitch is numbered in green. Always bring needle up through the canvas at odd numbers and take it back down through the canvas at the even numbers.

Background Stitches

The following stitches are used for filling in large areas of canvas. The Continental Stitch is the most commonly used stitch. Other stitches, such as the Condensed Mosaic and Scotch Stitch, fill in large areas of canvas more quickly than the Continental Stitch because their stitches cover a larger area of canvas.

Continental Stitch
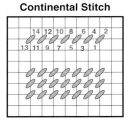

Condensed Mosaic
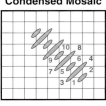

Alternating Continental
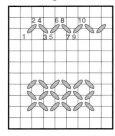

Cross Stitch
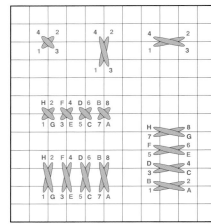

Long Stitch

Scotch Stitch

Slanting Gobelin

Embroidery Stitches

These stitches are worked on top of a stitched area to add detail to the project. Embroidery stitches are usually worked with one strand of yarn, several strands of pearl cotton or several strands of embroidery floss.

Lattice Stitch
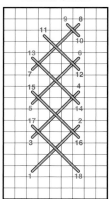

Chain Stitch
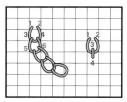

Couching
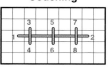

Straight Stitch
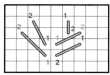

Running Stitch

Fly Stitch

Backstitch
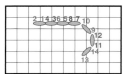

Embroidery Stitches

French Knot

Bring needle up through canvas. Wrap yarn around needle 1 to 3 times, depending on desired size of knot; take needle back through canvas through same hole.

Lazy Daisy

Bring yarn needle up through canvas, then back down in same hole, leaving a small loop. Then, bring needle up inside loop; take needle back down through canvas on other side of loop.

Loop Stitch/Turkey Loop Stitch

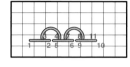

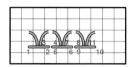

The top diagram shows this stitch left intact. This is an effective stitch for giving a project dimensional hair. The bottom diagram demonstrates the cut loop stitch. Because each stitch is anchored, cutting it will not cause the stitches to come out. A group of cut loop stitches gives a fluffy, soft look and feel to your project.

Specialty Stitches

The following stitches can be worked either on top of a previously stitched area or directly onto the canvas. Like the embroidery stitches, these too add wonderful detail and give your stitching additional interest and texture.

Satin Stitches

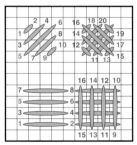

Smyrna Cross

Finishing Stitches

Overcast/Whipstitch

Overcasting and Whipstitching are used to finish the outer edges of the canvas. Overcasting is done to finish one edge at a time. Whipstitching is used to stitch two or more pieces of canvas together along an edge. For both Overcasting and Whipstitching, work one stitch in each hole along straight edges and inside corners, and two or three stitches in outside corners.

Lark's Head Knot

The Lark's Head Knot is used for a fringe edge or for attaching a hanging loop.

Buyer's Guide

When looking for a specific material, first check your local craft and retail stores and the Internet. If you are unable to locate a product, contact the manufacturers listed below for the closest retail source in your area or a mail-order source.

Coats & Clark Inc.
(800) 648-1479
www.coatsandclark.com

Darice
Mail-order source:
Schrock's International
P.O. Box 538
Bolivar, OH 44612
(800) 426-4659

DMC Corp.
(800) 275-4117
www.dmc-usa.com

Elmore-Pisgah Inc.
(800) 633-7829
www.elmore-pisgah.com

Kreinik Mfg. Co. Inc.
(800) 537-2166
www.kreinik.com

Lion Brand Yarn Co.
(800) 258-9276
www.lionbrand.com

Patons Yarns
(888) 368-8401
www.patonsyarns.com

Rainbow Gallery
(818) 982-4496
www.rainbowgallery.com

Toner Plastics
(413) 789-1300
www.tonerplastics.com

Uniek
Mail-order source:
Annie's Attic
(800) 282-6643
www.anniesattic.com

Wichelt Imports Inc.
(800) 356-9516
www.millhill.com